Blurred

A Daughter's Journey of Caregiving, Collapse, and Rediscovery

Tahnya Brown

Published by Tahn & Co LLC www.tahnco.com

ISBN: 979-8-9950372-0-0 (paperback)

ISBN: 979-8-9950372-1-7 (ebook)

First Edition: May 2026

Printed in the United States of America

Cover design by Tahnya Brown Cover art by Svitlana Stefaniuk

Edited by Elise Smith and Carmen Riot Smith, Wordy Wives

Dedication

In loving memory of my dad, a gentle, kind, and loving soul. Your resilience in the face of life's challenges, your constant thirst for knowledge, and the kindness you shared with everyone around you inspire me every day. This journey, and this book, are as much yours as they are mine.

Contents

Acknowledgments

I wrote this book after the caregiving ended. When the house grew quiet, I finally had the space to sit with all of it. The good. The bad. The utterly exhausting. The unexpectedly beautiful.

It poured out in pieces, shaped by memory and reflection, and stitched together with equal parts truth and tenderness.

To my best friend, Ninette, you've walked beside me through some of the darkest and most defining moments of my life. Your presence, perspective, and unwavering support have been a lifeline. You are like a sister, and your love and loyalty have held me up when I couldn't hold myself. This book carries your imprint. Thank you for being a huge part of my life.

To my family and friends, thank you for allowing me to share pieces of our story and for walking through the hard parts with me. I hope these pages reflect the depth of love behind every decision I made.

To the women I've coached, cried with, laughed with, and learned from. You were the mirror I didn't know I needed. Your undeniable strength inspired this work. You showed me that we are never truly alone when we tell the truth about what we carry.

To my team of supporters, creatives, and editors. You turned fragments into flow. Thank you for believing in this vision and helping me bring it to life with heart, clarity, and integrity.

To the caregivers, dreamers, survivors, and warriors who found themselves in these pages, I wrote this for you. May this book be a reminder that your story matters. That your strength is not invisible. And that you deserve joy, not just on the other side of pain, but right in the middle of it.

And finally, to the younger me, the girl who became the orchestrator, the fixer, the one who stepped in when things fell apart, who learned that control could keep the ground solid when nothing else would: You were never too much. You were exactly what we needed. Those traits weren't flaws. They were armor. They were preparation. Thank you for building me into someone who could handle this. Thank you for refusing to be anything less than strong.

With deep love and eternal gratitude,

Tahnya

Remember

She remembered who she was
not all at once,
but in the quiet spaces she once gave away.
In the silence after the noise.
In the breath after the battle.
And in that remembering, she rose.
To the woman who gives everything:
May you never again forget yourself.
May rest find you gently.
May joy call your name.
And may your next chapter
be written in your own voice
clear, unwavering, and free.

Prologue

Tonight, the moon is too full. Too present in the room. It pours silver through the windows and spreads across the floor like evidence. A year ago, it lit my father's bedroom the same way, tracing the outline of the bed where he took his last steady breaths.

I didn't understand what I was seeing then.

I do now.

The house is quiet but not peaceful. Quiet is only sound with its shoes off. Memory still walks where it wants.

I sit with a glass of wine in a room I designed to feel calm. Clean lines. Soft chairs. Intentional order. Space arranged by someone trying to contain grief instead of drowning in it. The mirror across from me catches a slanted reflection. I look ragged at the edges. Half-rendered. In progress.

The fatigue runs deeper now. Sleep doesn't touch it. It lives in bone and stays there. The parts of me that once planned, reached, and imagined feel distant, like rooms I no longer enter.

When the whisper comes, it isn't sound. It's recognition.

Write it down.

My father's voice, exactly as it always was when he meant something. Direct. Certain. No wasted words. The same voice that taught me to tie my shoes, question authority, and speak clearly even when it cost me. Strength was his curriculum.

He never taught me how to endure losing him. He assumed I would work that out myself.

This is where the story begins. Not at the first diagnosis or the first crisis. At the moment truth refuses burial.

Caregiving didn't ask me. It took. It redefined me without permission. It blurred the line between devotion and depletion and rewrote my days without negotiation.

Love became logistics, vigilance, and timing. Devotion became measurement. Did he eat? Did he sleep? Did he wander? Did I miss anything?

It also exposed what couldn't carry its weight.

My marriage was supposed to involve a shared holding. Mutual strain. Reinforcement. We were two people in the same structure under different gravity. He was present in the room, absent in the load. The difference became obvious when my worst days echoed back empty.

I didn't see how much of myself was disappearing while I managed the appointments. The daily meds. The meals. The middle-of-the-night checks. Everything that kept him alive and me running on empty.

Erosion works silently. Function remains. Essence drains.

These pages hold what happened in unseen spaces. Midnight systems. Unspoken negotiations. Competence built over fear. Private bargains to get through another day.

They also hold what remained.

The part of me that stayed awake through it all. Not loud. Not heroic. But constant. Waiting for the day I could step forward again.

The moon always knows.

And now, so do I.

Chapter 1

3:00 Am

Spring mornings came early. I dragged myself downstairs before the sun finished rising, the air already warm through the windows. Exhaustion hit hard. I hadn't slept at all. I stared at my coffee like it might save me, briefly considered getting it as an IV drip, then sent Darius to Starbucks for a double espresso and waited.

When he got back, I wrapped both my hands around it. The heat pressed through my fingers and into my chest, and for one breath, nothing else existed.

My mind picked up exactly where it had left off. Frustrated, overwhelmed, buzzing with adrenaline that had nowhere to go.

I moved through the day on autopilot. Meds. Meals. Damage control.

By dinner, I was running on fumes. The day had been a war of small refusals and constant redirections, every hour demanding more than I had left to give.

That night.

It was uneventful. Almost too easy.

He ate what I put in front of him without complaint, as he sometimes did when the day hadn't demanded too much of him. I watched him closely, always learning the difference between calm and compliance, between cooperation and peace.

After dinner, I stood up and opened the freezer.

"How about some ice cream, Dad?" I asked.

He nodded. "Yeah. That sounds good."

Ice cream had become part of the routine. Not because he asked for it, but because he refused medication outright. Pills were a hard no. No swallowing. No negotiating. So, I adapted.

I had ordered a pill grinder made specifically for that purpose, the one people use when swallowing becomes a battle. I ground his medication carefully, making sure it was fine enough to disappear completely, then mixed it into the ice cream. The routine had some give. Sometimes I mixed it into pudding. Sometimes applesauce. Tonight, ice cream.

One of the pills was meant to help him sleep.

I was extra meticulous with that one.

I stirred deliberately, watching the powder dissolve, making sure there were no clumps, no residue left behind. I handed him the bowl at the kitchen table and stayed close as he ate, pretending to tidy up while my eyes tracked every bite.

This was part of it now. The unspoken negotiations. The strategies that looked gentle from the outside and were anything but.

Care delivered through vigilance. Love measured by whether the bowl came back empty.

When he finished, I double-checked it, just to be sure.

Clean.

"Good," I said, more to myself than to him.

Later, I helped him get ready for bed. Fresh pajamas. Teeth brushed. Lights dimmed. I walked him down the hall and waited until he was settled, the covers pulled up just right, his breathing already slowing.

"You okay?" I asked.

"Yeah," he said. "I'm okay."

I stood there longer than necessary, scanning the room as I always did. Doors. Floor. Corners. Nothing out of place. Nothing wrong.

I turned off the light and closed the door halfway. I went downstairs and checked everything again.

Back door locked.

Mancave locked.

Front door locked.

Garage door locked.

Alarm on. Cameras set.

Nothing about that night felt different.

That's what gets me.

I don't remember falling asleep. Just the sense that everything was finally contained. I sank into bed, wrapped in covers, letting myself believe in the protection I had built.

I thought about the alarm company rep earlier that day, standing in my kitchen, nodding approvingly.

"Great setup," he'd said. "Nothing's getting in here without a big show."

"It's not someone getting in," I told him. "I'm worried about someone getting out."

He'd paused, confused, until I explained about my father. The dementia. The wandering.

I drifted asleep believing the house was secure. Believing he was safe. That belief followed me down into the first real sleep I'd had in days, one I desperately needed, and I let myself rest inside it.

Sleep had just taken me when the alarm ripped through the house.

Loud.

Violent.

I shot up in bed, my heart slamming against my ribs, pulse flooding my neck, body already bracing as I forced my eyes open.

Red numbers on the wall flashed into focus.

3:00 *a.m.*

The blare hit my chest before I could make sense of it. I threw my hands over my ears, my whole body vibrating against the noise. My feet landed on the floor before my mind caught up.

And then it hit me.

Holy FUCK!

The alarms.

He's OUT!

That thought cut through the blaring haze like a knife.

I bolted from bed, adrenaline flooding my system. The familiar rush of panic. Not blind this time, like that first escape, but calculated panic, colder somehow, more gripping.

I had planned for this. I had prepared for this.

I had locked every damn door.

So how the hell did he get out?!

Darius and I tore through the house, checking doors and windows.

The back door. Locked.

The garage. Locked.

Mancave. Locked.

Then I saw it.

The front door.

Wide open.

I froze, my brain refusing to accept what my eyes were seeing. There was no way he got out this time.

No way he had beaten the locks, the alarms, the security.

But he had.

And now, he was gone.

Panic tumbled into action.

I threw on my slippers, grabbed my car keys with hands I couldn't control, and bolted outside.

The darkness swallowed me whole.

The air was thick with suffocating silence.

And somewhere out there was my father.

But this time I didn't call 911. I knew his route now. I knew his pattern. I knew he was walking home. Except "home" was miles away, decades ago, in another state.

I jumped in my car and sped off into the night, my eyes scanning every shadow, my hands gripping the wheel so hard I could feel my nails in my skin.

And then I saw him.

A small figure in the distance.

Moving in the middle of the street.

Heading straight toward a major intersection.

I hit the gas and closed the distance, whipping the car in front of him, throwing it into park so fast the tires screeched.

I jumped out.

"Dad!" I said, gasping, barely aware I'd been clenching every muscle in my body.

He turned, looking at me like nothing was wrong.

Like we weren't in the middle of the damn road at 3 a.m.

"Oh, hey, how ya doin?" He waved like he was happy to find a ride.

I rushed toward him, ready to grab him, to drag him into the car if I had to.

As I reached for him, everything lit up.

Flashing lights.

A siren blasted, its cacophony of blue and red flooding the street.

A cop.

For a split second, my brain short-circuited.

Shit.

They think I'm drunk.

I must've looked erratic—a woman in a nightgown and slippers, stopping her car in the middle of the street, frantically reaching for an old man.

But the miraculous happened.

The officer stepped forward, looked at my father, and understood.

He didn't reach for his gun.

He didn't demand an explanation.

He didn't treat us like a crime scene.

Instead, he looked at me.

"Ma'am, is this your dad?"

I exhaled so hard I almost collapsed.

"Yes. Yes. He has dementia. I—he got out. I didn't—"

My words fell out faster than I could shape them.

The officer nodded.

"Let's get him home."

And then, like an angel disguised in a badge, he asked one small, life-saving question:

"Have you heard of Project Lifesaver?"

I hadn't.

He reached into his pocket and handed me a business card.

"This is the lead officer who runs the program in our area," he said. "They work with families dealing with wandering. They can get him set up with a tracking device."

I stared at the card, my fingers barely able to hold it, choking back tears.

I had been searching for answers, help, any way to keep my father safe. And this officer, this complete stranger, had just handed me exactly what I needed.

The following day, I called the number. For the first time since this nightmare began, I didn't feel alone. The officers in charge of Project Lifesaver were kind, patient, and understanding. They didn't just treat my father as "another case." They treated us like a family in crisis. A family that needed help.

Within days, they fitted my father with a GPS tracking bracelet. If he got out again, I wouldn't have to call 911. I wouldn't have to search blindly in the dark. I wouldn't have to wonder if I would find him in time. I had a direct line to the people who could find him within minutes.

These officers, these men and women I had never met before, became part of my caregiving team. They became a resource that gave me back a fraction of myself.

That night, in the middle of that road, as my father climbed into my car, as if nothing had happened, I knew the officer wasn't just some cop. He was sent there by a force bigger than me. Bigger than chance.

I glanced at Dad as we headed back home. He was relaxed and smiling, untouched by the night.

I wasn't. I was carrying every second of it.

And somewhere between the street and the driveway, it became the truth I could no longer outrun.

No version of my life didn't look like this now.

No exit.

No pause.

No one coming to relieve me.

Chapter 2

The Gleam of New Beginnings

It was 2015, five years before my father moved in.

Before any of this began.

Before caregiving had a face. An address. A 3 a.m. alarm.

The air was warm, wrong for December in upstate New York, like winter had forgotten us for a day. I sat in my car with the engine ticking, answering emails to keep my hands busy while I waited. My heart was a mix of happy, nervous, and a tension I didn't want to name. I stepped out, my heels clicking against the sidewalk, too loud for the emptiness around me, as I walked toward the attorney's office. The walk stretched longer than it should have. I tugged my coat tighter even though the air was unseasonably off.

My stomach was fluttering. That tickle it does when my wager is big.

Inside, the building smelled like peppermint and furniture polish layered over what came before it—wood, paper, decades of contracts signed and filed. Garland draped the walls in loose swags. White lights blinked in the corners like they were already tired of the season. A secretary sat at the front desk, tidying stacks of paper with the desperate energy of someone counting down to vacation. She glanced up when I walked past, smiled politely, and went back to her work.

The attorney looked up when I stepped into his office. My agent was already seated at the conference table, folder open, pen in hand.

"Ready?" the attorney asked, standing to shake my hand.

"The Johnsons already signed," my agent added, gesturing to the chair beside him. "Shouldn't take more than thirty minutes."

I nodded and sat down, setting my purse on the seat beside me. The chair was leather—good leather that didn't creak. The conference table was cherry, polished to a shine that caught the overhead lights and threw them back at me in warm, distorted reflections.

Pages slid toward me one at a time. I read every line, even though I'd already read them twice before. The attorney's voice became background noise as he walked through clauses I'd already memorized. Pen clicked. Signature looped across the bottom. Next page. Pen clicked. Signature looped.

My hand moved without hesitation, even though my chest was tight.

On the final page, I capped my pen and slid the folder forward across the table. The sound of paper against wood seemed louder than it should have been.

No more flutter in my chest. No second guess.

I'd done this before in 2001, with nothing but pay stubs and a spine made of grit. Fresh off my divorce from my first husband, Brianna and Collin's father, buying the townhouse next to my parents like I was daring the world to bet against me. And I won. That house became my proving ground. Small. Manageable. Mine.

This one was different.

The house was bigger. The bet bolder. And this time, Darius was here.

Not my husband. Not yet. Not on paper. We'd tried marriage once, and it hadn't held. But here we were, beside each other again, offering to try one more time. He'd brought part of the down payment. I'd brought the history of holding things together. For once, it was like we were stepping into life side by side instead of me dragging us both forward.

The attorney shook my hand again, then Darius'. My agent gathered the paperwork into a neat stack and tucked it into his briefcase with a satisfied click of the latches.

"Congratulations," he said, smiling. "You're a homeowner."

I thanked him, grabbed my purse, and walked back outside to the air of December pretending to be April.

When we pulled into the driveway, we didn't rush inside. We paused, staring up at it.

The house sat back from the street, bigger than anything I'd owned before. The late afternoon light hit the windows at an angle, turning them gold. The yard stretched wide on both sides, green grass, despite the season.

I unlocked the front door, pushed it open, and let the sound echo.

"Wow," Darius said from behind me.

We walked through it once. Without rushing. Wide rooms opened into wider rooms. High ceilings made our footsteps sound hollow. Thirty-five hundred square feet, both grand and unfinished, like a stage waiting for the show to start.

The kitchen stopped me.

Cherry cabinets climbed all the way to the ceiling, dark and polished, the grain catching the light in waves. The chrome refrigerator gleamed against the far wall, untouched. The air carried the sharp bite of ammonia and the waxy sweetness of furniture polish. Someone had scrubbed this place clean before handing over the keys.

I ran my hand along the bare counters and pressed my palm flat against the cool granite.

"This kitchen is ridiculous."

"Mm-hmm." His hands stayed in his coat pockets.

"Let's take a selfie." I pulled out my phone.

He stepped in behind me without hesitation, that Darius smile already in place.

"Say cheese!"

I snapped the photo, checked it, and took another just to be sure.

We moved through the rest of the house, room by room, every sound bouncing off bare walls. I pointed out what would go where. Couch here. Table there. The bedroom centered around that window.

He followed a few steps behind me, hands in his pockets, taking it in without saying much. I kept glancing back at him.

"You good?" I turned to face him.

"Yeah." That same wide grin—his answer for everything.

I turned back to the room and kept talking. Slowing down. Filling the space between us with plans, with details, with ideas he didn't seem to need. But this time, he was beside me. Not behind. Not elsewhere. Right here. I made sure he was in it.

By the time we finished, the sun had set completely. The house went dark except for the glow from the wood stove we'd lit in the corner of the living room.

We unpacked the cheap air mattress from its crinkly plastic, the pump whining as it filled. We laid down, side by side in our coats for the night, too tired to dig through boxes for blankets. The movers were coming at six the next morning—Christmas Eve day.

The wood stove crackled and popped, pushing warmth into empty corners.

I pulled out my phone and posted our selfie from earlier. The two of us lit by the kitchen's glow, cabinets shining behind us as proof the bet paid off. *New beginnings*, I wrote on the post.

The comments came fast. Hearts. Congratulations. Variations of *you two look happy*.

I showed him the screen.

"Look at that," I said, showing him the post. "Everyone thinks we've got it figured out."

"Maybe we do," he said.

I stared at the photo for a long time before putting my phone down.

"Are you happy?"

"Yeah," he said, turning his head to look at me. "I really am."

"Me too."

And I meant it.

Lying there in the dark, listening to the fire fade, I could already see it. Mornings in that kitchen. Dinner around a table that didn't exist yet. A house that finally felt like ours. Like maybe, this time, we'd get it right.

I closed my eyes and let the warmth wrap around us.

Darius's breathing slowed beside me—long, low exhales that pressed into the silence like he'd already forgotten the weight of the day

My eyes grew heavy. And for the first time in years, I let myself believe it.

That we could make this work.

That the future we were building was real.

Chapter 3

Proof In Motion

Christmas Eve arrived, sunny, warm, and bright.

The movers arrived before I'd finished my coffee, their truck grumbling up the driveway just after six. Wearing my sweatshirt from the night before, mug in hand, I started running the scene like a meeting.

"Back an inch. Angle left. Watch the banister."

Control was my comfort language.

"Chair there," I said, pointing to the wall opposite the windows. "Loveseat across from it. And the dining table anchors that wall."

They landed it right on the first try. I clapped once.

Boxes stacked up like short city blocks against the walls. Darius helped, placing each one in the designated room I'd labeled in thick black marker.

I moved through the open rooms in my socks, flipping switches, figuring out what controlled what. Hall lights turned on bedroom fixtures. Doubles that did nothing. A switch near the back door seemed to control an outlet I couldn't find.

I flipped them again. And again. Click by click, waiting for one of them to answer.

Mapping it all. Making it make sense.

By the second pass, I had it sorted. Not just the fixtures, but which walls needed paint, which rooms caught the morning light, and which went dim until afternoon.

Collin came in from his friend's house, dropped his bag at the door, and headed straight upstairs like he already owned the place.

"This one's mine," he called down. "I'm putting all my sneakers in those cubbies."

I looked upstairs. "It's yours. Keep it clean!"

We had room for everyone who might need it. No aunt on a sofa. No niece in a sleeping bag. No, "I'll take the floor." Dignity, by design.

My family was already making their way up from downstate to celebrate Christmas together. By noon, the front door had turned into a bellows. Open. Shut. Open. Shut. Fresh air pushing through with every arrival.

My mother came first, struggling through the door with two suitcases and an armful of Christmas bags that threatened to spill.

"Tahnya, where do you want these?" she called, flushed, cheeks pink from the unseasonably warm air.

"Counter in the kitchen is fine for now," I said, steering a lamp around a stack of boxes without looking up.

"Okay, but it's going to drive you crazy sitting there," she warned, already heading that direction.

"Everything drives me crazy," I said. "I'll live."

She laughed and disappeared into the kitchen.

My father followed a few steps behind, carrying a bag of paper towels in one hand and more presents in the other. He stopped just inside the door, eyes wide, head tilting back to take in the size of the rooms.

"This is huge," he said, his voice close to awe. "You've outdone yourself."

I smiled, wiping dust off my hands onto my jeans. "You taught me that if I'm going to do something, do it right."

He chuckled. "Well, you certainly did it right."

I watched him take it in. His eyes swept the rooms methodically, left to right, like he was trying to memorize the layout. He paused at doorways. Looked down hallways. Turned in a slow circle. A part of me filed that look away. Stored it. I didn't know why yet.

Nadene came through the door next with her daughter right behind her, already mid-sentence, my niece smiling, hugging me, and carrying her bag upstairs to find Collin.

"Do you have a spot for our stuff?" Nadene dropped her bags at the bottom of the stairs.

"Upstairs," I said, pointing toward the staircase.

"Which room?"

"Any with a bed."

"Not the couch!" she laughed, already halfway up the stairs.

"There is no couch sleeping in this house. EVER." I winked at my niece.

"Fancy," Nadene called back, singing down at me from the landing. "We've moved on up to the eastside."

The voices multiplied after that. The upstairs hall became a drum, feet pounding against carpet that muffled nothing. Doors opened and closed. Laughter from one room. A yell about a bathroom from another.

I walked my father to the top of the stairs and tied a single balloon to the doorknob of the room I'd chosen for him. Silver. Shiny. The house was big enough to get lost in. The balloon bobbed in the draft from the heating vent, catching light from the hallway.

"This one's yours," I told him, pushing the door open so he could see inside. "Mom's is next door."

He nodded.

They hadn't shared a bed in as long as I could remember. No one explained. No one needed to.

He glanced once more at the balloon, fingers brushing it lightly, so it spun on its string, then stepped inside.

I heard the front door open downstairs.

"Hello!" Brianna's voice carried through the house before she did. "Merry Christmas, everybody!"

She came through the door with gift bags in both hands, hugged me quick and tight, and walked straight into the kitchen. She lived ten minutes away, but this was her first time seeing the house.

"Mom. This kitchen is insane."

"I know."

She set the bags on the counter and took off to explore the rest of the house.

"Do I get a room?"

"Sure," I giggled. "Pick one."

I lingered in the hallway for a moment, listening to the house fill around me. Voices downstairs. Movement overhead. The furnace kicking on with a low rumble.

"Where's the tree?" My mother's voice cut through from downstairs. She took Christmas seriously. Required all the pomp and circumstance of the holiday.

"At the lot with all the other trees," I called back. "And that's where it'll stay. Not this year."

I didn't give her room to question further. The thought of trying to wrestle a tree into this chaos was beyond impossible. Ornaments and lights were packed away somewhere in a plastic bin labeled "HOLIDAY."

That night, we all drove to my cousin's house and gathered around their tree. My house sat waiting behind us, bare and half-arranged. But it breathed. And upstairs, six beds waited for six people who wouldn't have to say, "Don't worry, I'll take the couch."

That was my gift. Proof of love in linen and slats.

I'd never had that before. I grew up in a three-bedroom townhouse where company meant someone on the pullout couch and someone else in a sleeping bag on the floor. There was a trundle bed somewhere. We made it work because we always made it work.

My first house after my divorce from their father had the same footprint — just my kids and me filling the rooms. Then Darius and I married in 2004, and we made that house a home. Until we didn't. After the divorce, I moved north with Collin. Bri decided to stay. An apartment in upstate New York. Big enough for Collin and me, not big enough for anyone else.

This time, every room had a purpose. Every bed already made. No shifting. No rearranging. No one waiting to see where they'd land.

Everything already decided.

For the first time, no one had to think about it.

The holiday passed as holidays do when the house is full — too fast, too loud, and over before anyone's ready. Soon, we were waving goodbye as my family headed back downstate, and the house returned to its own silence.

I watched them pull out of the driveway that day and waved until I couldn't see the car anymore. It didn't cross my mind that my dad would be back.

That one day, this house wouldn't just be a place he visited.

That one day, it would be his.

There was nothing to read. No sign to catch. He was just my dad, taking his time through my house as he took his time through everything. Unhurried. Present. Pausing at doorways like he wanted to remember them.

I walked into the kitchen, bare feet cold against the tile, nudging the coffee maker where it belonged—pushed it back against the wall—shifted it a fraction of an inch to the left. Then back again. Perfect. Mine to control.

Darius came in with an empty box, flattened and folded under one arm, waiting for direction.

"Garage," I said.

He nodded once and took it out.

The dishwasher sloshed in the background. The fridge kicked on with a low groan. Outside, a car drove past, headlights sweeping across the living room wall.

The house had become home.

Later, when the faucets stopped dripping, and the ducts stopped creaking, and the house found its night sound, I lay in bed. Hands behind my head. Eyes on the ceiling, I'd chosen. White. Clean. Mine.

Down the hall, Dad's balloon, tied to the doorknob, tapping rhythmic and faithful, like a heartbeat.

I lay there listening, absorbing what the house now carried from a single day. The sound of pans clinking in the kitchen. My mother's voice asking where things went, mine snapping back. Nadene doubled over laughing at Brianna and Collin, who had the whole room in stitches with their back-and-forth. My niece watching from the corner, grinning, waiting to drop one of her zingers. My father in doorways, taking it all in with that intent, measured attention.

The house was big enough for all of it.

Summer was already set in my mind.

And I couldn't wait for it to get here.

Chapter 4

Clockwork

The house had its own morning routine by now—two months in, and I knew it by heart. The furnace kicked on first, then the pipes gurgled awake, pushing heat through the walls like a pulse. I was awake already, watching the light slip through the blinds, brushing across the counter where I'd lined up the day: keys, phone, purse, bills. Upstairs came the familiar sounds of movement, drawers opening, water running, the muffled thud of sneakers against carpet.

"Collin," I called. "Jersey, water bottle, backpack. Don't forget anything."

"I got it," he said, his voice thick with sleep and a dash of annoyance. Seconds later, he came bounding down the stairs, all long limbs and energy, his hoodie half-zipped and earbuds hanging around his neck.

"You're cutting it close again," I said.

"The bus will wait," he said, grinning like he already knew it wouldn't.

"It never does."

He laughed, that half-boy, half-man sound, already partially out the door. "Five-ten for warm-ups," I called after him. His hand went up in a backward wave.

"Got it," he said, the front door closing behind him.

A few minutes later, Darius came down, unhurried as always. In his typical jeans and sweater. The perfect business casual look. He grabbed an iced tea in one hand and a banana in the other.

"You headed in now?" I asked.

He nodded. "Gotta get in early. Testing a new system today."

"Drive safe," I said, glancing up from the sink, waiting for my morning peck on the cheek.

"Will do." He peeled the banana with one hand, his mind already somewhere else. "You good?"

"I'm good," I said.

He tossed the peel in the trash, set his drink on the counter, and leaned in to kiss me. "See you tonight."

"Text me when you're on your way home."

"Will do," he answered, already out the door.

The house went silent. I lingered there for a moment, my coffee cooling on the counter, looking out the window at the backyard. The deck light was left on overnight, haloed in mist. The fence leaned slightly where winter had warped the post. Some part of me always noticed what needed fixing, what tilted, what could be made right again.

I finished my coffee, rinsed the mug, and headed upstairs to get ready.

By the time I reached the office, Monday was already underway. I worked in financial services, moving through branches, developing teams, and improving performance across locations. It was work I was good at and work I loved.

I pushed open the glass doors into the low murmur of conversation and keyboards clicking, and my team greeted me with that familiarity we'd built over the years.

"Good morning, everyone," I said, setting my bag down. "How we doing? You all look like you've had a long week."

Laughter rippled through the room.

We dove into the meeting, notes spread across the table, laptops open. I asked questions, listened, and nudged.

"What's working? What are our biggest challenges?"

Seth, one of the analysts, mentioned a communication gap between shifts, and I nodded.

"Alright, that's fixable. Let's make it simpler for the next rotation. We're too good to lose time over things we can control."

Someone smiled. "You always make it sound easy."

"It's not that simple, it just looks that way when everyone's pulling together."

By the time our meeting wrapped, the room was lighter. Chairs scraped back, laptops clicked shut, and people drifted out in pairs until it was just me and Mariah still gathering our things.

"You alright?" I asked.

She nodded, papers tucked under her arm. "Just double-checking that I didn't miss anything. I still get nervous in these meetings."

"That's ok," I said. "You did great today."

Her shoulders eased. "You make it look effortless."

"It's not," I said with a smile. "It's just practice, and a good team." I glanced at the clock. "My son's got a basketball game. I've gotta head out before traffic hits."

Mariah smiled. "That sounds fun. He's lucky to have you cheering."

"I'm the loudest one there," I said, grabbing my coat.

She laughed. "Somehow I believe that."

I smiled back and started for the door. The hallway lights buzzed above me—that familiar pull between two lives, the one where I managed people and the one where I was somebody's mother.

The gym was already packed, whistles and shouts bouncing off the walls, the bleachers half-full of parents claiming their spots. Collin was already out there stretching, tall and focused, his movements smooth and precise. When the whistle blew, he was ready, a blur of motion and instinct.

"Let's go, Bubba!" I yelled, clapping from the stands.

He looked up just long enough to grin before sinking back into the game. That was our language. No big gestures, no words needed.

Afterward, the car filled with the smell of sweat and fries. "You played great," I said.

He shrugged. "I missed one I shouldn't have."

"Not a big deal," I said, smiling. "There's always next time."

He smirked, his face hidden behind the bag of fries.

"My word, you hungry?"

"Always." He shoveled a handful of fries into his mouth.

"I'll make dinner when we get home."

The porch light glowed across the driveway when we pulled in. I kicked off my heels at the door and headed straight to the kitchen. "What do you want for dinner?" I asked.

"Whatever's fast," Collin said, dropping his bag by the counter and scrolling through his phone.

"Then grab the plates," I said. "Go walk the dogs, please, and then get cleaned up."

I moved through the kitchen, all muscle memory: oil in the pan, a pinch of salt, a routine my body had practiced for years. The room filled with the sound of onions hitting the pan and Collin laughing as he tried to corral the dogs.

"You cooking?" Darius asked, coming into the kitchen, confirming what he already knew.

"Looks like it," I said. "Just throwing together some chicken and rice."

"Got it." He set his drink on the counter and watched while I stirred. "Smells good."

"Thank you," I said, flipping the chicken, letting it catch a little color before turning it again.

We ate together at the table, our conversation effortless. Collin told us about the game, about his teammate who tripped mid-play.

I laughed. "Well, did you help him?" I asked.

"Of course," he said. "Always."

Darius looked up. "Good, good," his words were warm and simple.

We finished, and Darius stood to start clearing the plates, stacking them neatly in the sink.

I leaned against the counter and watched him.

There is nothing quite like a handsome man who does the dishes without being asked.

He moved through the kitchen with purpose, rinsing, stacking, putting things back where they belonged. It was how he decompressed. How he loved. Not through declarations or grand gestures, but through action. I had chosen this man once before. Standing there watching him, I understood exactly why I was choosing him again.

"We should pick a date."

He turned slightly. "For what?"

"The wedding," I raised my hands in air quotes, "slash housewarming party."

He smiled. "You tell me when."

"I'm thinking June. Backyard. Family, friends, food, and fun."

He nodded. "Sounds good."

"I'll call my parents tomorrow."

He started rinsing the dishes. "They'll be happy for you."

"For us," I corrected softly.

He didn't answer, just gave a slight grin, turning back to the water running in the sink.

We didn't want a huge announcement. Not really. To everyone else, it would be a housewarming, a celebration of the new house, the new chapter, the fresh start. That part was true enough.

"We don't have to make it a big thing," he said.

"I don't want to," I agreed.

We both knew what people would think. We knew the questions that would come. Are you sure? Again? Didn't you already try this?

I didn't want to defend it. I didn't want gifts, obligations, or people snuffing out our hope like a candle before it had a chance to burn.

I just wanted us to begin again without an audience.

So, we kept it simple. Housewarming. Come celebrate the house. That was enough.

The next morning, before heading into work, I sat at the kitchen table and dialed my parents' number.

"Hey, Dad," I said.

"Hey, Tahn, what's up? How's it going?" he said, his voice warm and slow like always.

"We're good. Busy, but good."

There was a pause, just long enough to feel him listening.

"Listen," I said, lowering my voice like someone might over-hear. "I wanted to tell you something. Darius and I decided to get remarried."

He didn't speak right away, and then I heard the soft laugh in his voice. "Really? Oh, that's great!"

"Yeah. But we're keeping it quiet. It's going to look like a house-warming. Mom doesn't know."

He chuckled, already in on it. "You want me to keep it from her?"

"I do," I said. "If she finds out, she'll have it on Facebook before I hang up the phone."

That got him laughing harder. "You're right about that. Your mother and that Facebook. She never stays off that damn thing."

"Exactly," I said, smiling. "I want you to walk me down the proverbial aisle, like before."

His voice softened. "Okay. I think I am gonna need a suit or something."

"Yeah, I know. Darius said he would help you find one."

He let out a small sigh that almost sounded like pride. "I'm happy for you, Tahn. You always find a way to build your life the way you want it."

"I try."

"That's all any of us can do, and I won't tell your mother."

"I'm just going to tell her it is a housewarming party like we're telling everyone else."

After the call, I looked around the kitchen. The morning light had shifted just enough to catch the steam rising from my coffee mug.

Everything looked right. The house, the plans, the promise of our future. For the first time in a long time, nothing in me was bracing. Life had paused long enough to let me breathe.

I could already see it: The low murmur of guests, the glow of string lights along the deck, and my father waiting at the top of the stairs, hand outstretched, calm and certain. He'd flash that proud, knowing smile, the one that said he believed in me long before I ever did.

He would be there, watching me start again, proud that I'd built a life on my own terms. To everyone else, it would look like a celebration, but to me, it would be much more than that. A homecoming. A chance to say without words, *I'm okay, Dad. You did good.*

The thought of him there anchored me. Whatever came next, I knew the day would be beautiful. Not because of the vows or the house or the crowd, but because he'd be beside me. My dad, in his element, proud of his little girl.

Chapter 5

Fixed Joy

Rain pounded the roof that morning. Not a thin drizzle, but a heavy, confident summer rain that had turned the air thick and clean.

The wedding was set for eleven. Not that anyone knew it was a wedding yet.

My mother found out the night before.

"You should have told me." Her voice was tight with hurt. "I wouldn't have said anything."

I smirked, already turning away. "We both know that isn't true. You and Facebook tell the world everything."

She shook her head, offended but unable to argue. "You think you're so funny."

"I think I know my mother." No malice, just truth.

Upstairs, my father was already dressed. I overheard him and Darius laughing over one of Darius's silly comments.

"Fast Eddie, do you have a Band-Aid?"

"No, why? You need one?"

"Nah, I was thinking you might. You look so sharp you could cut yourself."

Chuckling, they made their way downstairs, and Darius headed outside to take his place under the tent.

When I appeared at the top of the stairs, my father turned toward me. He looked dapper in his suit, standing tall and proud. That smile broke wide across his face — the one that started in his eyes before his mouth caught up, the one that said he was in on something the rest of the world hadn't figured out yet. It was proof I was doing something right. That he knew it too.

"You ready, Tahn?" he asked.

My heart swelled. "I am."

"Okay, let's go then."

He took the umbrella leaning by the door, opened it, and held it high as we stepped outside. The rain had mostly stopped, but he held it above us anyway. We crossed the deck, the boards slick under our feet. I held onto his arm, my fingers wrapping into the sleeve of his suit.

When we reached the edge of the tent, I spotted Darius waiting at the other end.

His face changed the moment he saw us coming. His whole expression opened. That Darius smile spread wide, but his eyes were what got me. They were bright. Almost glassy. Like he was holding back tears but didn't want anyone to see.

He looked at me like I was the only person who mattered. Like this moment was everything he'd been waiting for.

The scent of wet grass and summer air wrapped around us as my father and I walked toward him. My heels sank slightly into the lawn while the last of the rain tapped gently on the canvas above. No crowd yet. No music. Just my friends, immediate family, and my father walking me into a new beginning, his hand steady as ever. I exhaled as I got closer to Darius.

We were really doing this. Again.

But this time felt different.

The first time, we were still figuring each other out. Learning how to communicate. How to navigate expectations. How to be partners instead of two people living side by side.

This time, we knew exactly what we were walking into. We'd already failed once. We'd already walked away. And here we were, choosing each other again anyway.

Not because it was simple. Because we fit. He was patient. I was fire. He was present. I was relentless. Together, we worked.

And standing there, approaching Darius in his gray suit, salt-and-pepper beard trimmed close, looking distinguished and completely at ease, waiting for me under that tent, I believed it completely.

I looked at my father. His eyes were full of pride, fixed on me like he'd been waiting his whole life for this exact second. He squeezed my hand once, then placed it in Darius's.

"Take care of her," he said quietly.

Darius nodded, his voice thick. "I will."

My father stepped back, and it was just the two of us standing there, hands joined, eyes locked.

The officiant began to speak, but I barely heard the words. I was too focused on Darius's face. The way he was looking at me. The way his thumb brushed across my knuckles, tracing slow circles, as if slowed down for just the two of us.

When it was time for vows, his voice was confident.

"You are the strongest woman I know," he said, his eyes never leaving mine. "Beautiful, smart, driven. You don't need me to complete you. You never did."

He smiled, that genuine warmth spreading across his face.

"But I want to be the one standing beside you anyway. Supporting you. Loving you. Being your partner in all of it."

His voice pulling inward, just enough.

"You deserve someone who sees you. Who appreciates everything you are. And I promise to be that man. Every day."

My throat tightened. Tears spilled over before I could stop them.

When it was my turn, I smiled through them.

"I promise to make this house a home," I said. "To fill it with love and laughter and all the chaos that comes with our life together."

I paused, grinning at him, then looked out at our friends and family.

"And I solemnly vow to never, ever touch the laundry."

Laughter erupted. Darius threw his head back.

"Ever," I repeated, squeezing his hands. "That's your domain, and I love you for it."

He pulled me close, chuckling, wrapping his arms around me tightly. I felt the warmth of his chest against mine, felt him press his face against my temple.

"I love you," he whispered, just for me.

"I love you too."

When we finally pulled apart, the small crowd around us erupted in applause. My father was smiling, pride in his eyes. My mother was beaming, happy we were back together. My friends were clapping and sharing in our joy.

We kissed one more time, and the officiant pronounced us husband and wife.

I looked at the small gathering under the tent. It was perfect. Intimate. Exactly what I had envisioned. Just us and the people who mattered most. Nothing spectacular or over the top. Me in a simple cream dress. Darius, in his gray suit looking handsome and relaxed.

By the time our ceremony finished, the clouds had fully lifted, and light poured through the open sides of the tent, touching everything with hues of gold. Inside the house, the cake sat waiting for the celebration to begin. Two tiers, white and gold, topped with *Mr. & Mrs.*

By one o'clock, more guests began to arrive. Shorts and T-shirts. Gift bags. Chatting and laughing. I stepped out onto the front porch to greet them, excitement in my eyes, Darius beside me with his inviting smile and warm hugs for everyone.

"Wow," a friend said, pausing on the porch. "This house is huge."

"It's beautiful, Tahnya."

Pride caught in my chest. This house. This life. We'd built it piece by piece. And now it was alive with voices, with love, with possibility.

As guests moved inside, their expressions began to shift. Those who came for a housewarming caught sight of my cream dress. Noticed Darius in his suit. Then the two-tiered cake, centered on the dining room table, its gold accents gleaming.

Confusion flickered first. Then curiosity. Then pure delight.

"Hold on," Kate, our neighbor, said, her eyes widening. "Did you two just get married?"

I clinked my glass to hers. "We did!"

The words set off a wave of recognition. Every few minutes, someone else caught on. Surprise blooming into joy, laughter bubbling over itself. "You're kidding!" "No way!" "You really did it!"

This. This was what I wanted. Not a performance. Just joy. Shared. Unplanned. Pure.

"You really pulled it off," one of my friends said, beaming. "This is so you."

"And sneaky," another added, laughing. "In the best possible way."

We clinked glasses, barely audible through the buzz of celebration and music.

It had been a long time since the future felt so full of promise.

Standing there, champagne in hand, surrounded by people I loved, I let myself imagine it. Not just the next year but the years beyond that. Growing old in this house. Waking up beside Darius every morning. Building my business. Watching my children create lives of their own. Celebrating more birthdays, more holidays, more ordinary, beautiful moments.

I imagined us twenty years from now, right here, still choosing each other, still laughing over dinner, still dancing in the kitchen when no one was watching.

That future had no uncertainty left in it.

The sound of familiar laughter pulled me back to my present. I spotted my father standing near the edge of the tent, talking with my uncle and watching the party unfold. His jacket had loosened, and his tie hung a little off-center. But he looked more himself that way. Comfortable. Happy. Exactly where he belonged.

Darius crossed the grass toward him, grinning, phone in hand, already queuing a song up through the speaker by the deck. "Fast Eddie, you sure you're not gonna get out there and show us how it's done?"

Dad chuckled, eyes twinkling. "You gotta play something different. MY music."

The opening notes of *Ain't Too Proud To Beg* by The Temptations came through the speakers, and Dad's whole body changed.

Alive. Electric. Free.

"Now that's more like it," Dad said, sliding one foot, then the other, shoulders rolling with rhythm.

He moved toward the center of the tent, where the tables had been pushed back to make room, and the crowd cheered. People stepping in around him.

I laughed, shaking my head, glancing at Darius. "See, you started something now."

Dad looked back at me, smiling wide and gave me a wink. Pure joy on his face. "This is how we had fun back in the day."

Darius joined him. Smooth but reserved. The two of them moving side by side, my father showing him steps he hadn't pulled out in years. The whole tent erupted.

My heart swelled watching them. This moment. My father so alive. So present. So himself.

When the song ended, he came over to me, breathing hard, eyes bright.

"You see that?" he said, riding the rhythm, "Still got it."

I stepped toward him, hand up, catching his in a high five. "You never lost it."

He nodded. "You did good, Tahn," his voice full of pride. "This is a great party."

"Thanks. It really turned out to be a great day. I'm proud and excited at the same time."

He looked at me a moment longer, a recognition passing between us. He saw what I didn't say out loud.

"You always were a strong one, and you always figure it out."

The words landed differently than he meant them.

Not praise.

Truth

He knew how much I carried. How much I held together. How much I hid. He'd always known.

As the music changed to *September* by Earth, Wind & Fire, he drifted back toward the tent, shaking hands, stopping to talk.

He looked like himself. Light. Charming.

And he was.

That day.

But I had seen other days. Days when things were just slightly off. His words would come out wrong, the cadence off, like a familiar song played in the wrong key. He wasn't angry. He was frustrated. Confused that no one could follow what made perfect sense to him. My mother would pull back, impatient, unwilling to meet him where he was. So I learned to step in. Decisively. This is what's happening, this is what we are doing. Make the call, handle what needed handling, and smooth what she couldn't bring herself to touch.

I had no words for it as a child. Just instinct. A knowing that arrived before the facts did.

Some daughters grow up learning to look pretty or behave.

I grew up learning how to be alert. How to read a room before anyone else knew there was something to read.

But watching him dance earlier, something in me knew better.

Moments like that don't stay still in my world.

Fastenings loosen.

Joy slips.

Chapter 6

Through the Doorway

Darius had the news on, remote in hand, searching for an episode of *Forensic Files*. It had been a full day, an ordinary one, and I sank into the couch, the dogs, Lola and Creed, not far behind. I grabbed a blanket and let them circle to get comfortable. Lola curled herself into a ball, and Creed sighed that long exhale that meant we were all finally at rest.

As the TV flickered, my eyes grew heavy. My hand rested on the nearest patch of fur, moving in slow, absent circles.

My mind drifted back. To a different house, decades ago.

Then the memory came, slipping in uninvited, switching the calm inside me before I had a chance to stop it.

It was dusk. I'd been outside most of the day, playing hard enough to leave grass stains on my knees and sun on my skin. I was curled up on my bed, my scruffy little dog, Miss Piggy, pressed against me like a second heartbeat. My world, in that instance, was small and safe. I heard the familiar sounds from downstairs. Pots clinking, my mother's voice rising and falling like background music. Everything normal.

But it wasn't.

The air changed first. A tension thick enough to notice but not yet name. My parents' voices became sharp, strange. My mother's clipped tone. My father's voice, lower than usual, with a current coiled beneath it.

And then he appeared.

He filled the doorway, blocking the light behind him. For a flicker of a second, he was still my father. And then, something shifted.

He held a book in his hand, speaking in a voice that didn't sound like his. It was flat and urgent. Distant. He wasn't angry. He wasn't loud. But he wasn't . . . there. Not the way he'd always been.

"Read it," he said. "You need to see. You need to know this stuff."

The words tumbled out, disjointed. Religion. Horses. An Indian. A vision. A prophecy. His mouth moved, but the meaning unraveled as it landed. I searched his eyes for anchor points, some trace of logic, comfort, connection. None of it lived there.

I wasn't afraid. Not in the way a child fears monsters under the bed. I was confused. Alert.

Something is wrong with my father.

It wasn't just a thought; it was a realization that took root deep in my chest, impossible to remove.

I didn't move, hoping the absence of movement would make the moment pass, but I was already rehearsing an escape.

Downstairs, my mother's voice rose: "Eddie! Come down here!"

He drifted back toward her voice, and I sprang into motion. I ran into my parents' room and grabbed my mother's blue oval cosmetic suitcase from her closet, the one she used for weekend getaways. I packed, my hands moving faster than my mind. Pajamas. Blanket. Pillow. Dog under one arm. Suitcase in the other.

I tiptoed down the stairs and slipped out the back door.

No shoes. Just instinct.

I ran to my best friend's house and banged on her door like the house was on fire, because inside me, it was. When her mother opened the door, I didn't even try to explain.

"Something's wrong with my dad," I said.

And she let me in.

Minutes later: sirens. Red and white lights painting the street. My father, being led to an ambulance, confused, resisting gently, his body not quite trusting the world anymore.

I stayed at my friend's house that night, watching from her kitchen window as the red and white lights faded down the street. My father was gone. Just like that.

He came home eventually. Stabilized. Medicated. Back to himself. Medication can do that, return someone to themselves, functional, present, recognizable. He went back to work. Back to being Dad.

Nobody said a word about it. Not my mother, not the neighbors, not anyone at school. This was the 1980s. You didn't talk about things like that. You especially didn't talk about them when the man in question was a respected RN who had spent thirty years helping other people get better.

It was the unspoken code of a small place where nothing stays fully hidden, but nobody crosses that line. Nobody called him crazy. Nobody made us feel uncomfortable.

He came home eventually. Days later, maybe more. No one sat me down to explain where he'd been or what had happened. My mother didn't offer it, and I didn't ask. That was how things worked in our house — difficult things dissolved into silence and life resumed its shape around them.

I remember visiting him once, at a place called Craig House in Beacon. A grand old building. Serious and grave. I didn't fully understand what it was then. I just knew it was where they took people when a part of them needed fixing.

Things went back to normal. Or what passed for normal. But I was different. I watched him differently from that night forward. Listened for shifts in his cadence. Waited for the air to change. I didn't yet have a name for what I'd seen in that doorway. I wouldn't for years.

But I knew what it felt like. And I never forgot it.

That was the night I learned the world could tilt without warning.

That safe wasn't permanent.

That I might have to be the one to act when things fell apart.

Creed against my leg, bringing me back as the TV flickered. Darius resting beside me, half asleep, a remote loose in his hand.

I stroked Lola's fur and let the memory recede where it lived.

I didn't talk about that night. Not to friends. Not even to myself most of the time.

But every choice I made after was shaped by it.

The need to stay alert. To see trouble before it arrived. To build structure strong enough that nothing could slip through the cracks.

That night taught me vigilance.

And vigilance, unchecked, becomes control.

Chapter 7

The Cracks

For years, I thought peace would look like those weeks and months following the wedding. The predictable routines. The order.

I had spent most of my life trying to outrun chaos, and when it finally stopped chasing me, I didn't know what to do with its nonexistence.

Somewhere inside, I was frequently reminded of the girl I became that night my father stood in the doorway, absent yet larger than life. The girl who learned to read danger in the air before anyone else noticed it. I didn't talk about her anymore, but she was still there, measuring each room she entered, keeping score, waiting for the next sign that something could fracture.

The alarm went off at 5:30 a.m. I reached for it before it could sound twice. Routine was my favorite form of control. It meant I could predict the next thing before it happened. Shower, lotion, clothes laid out, coffee brewed strong. Every step in its place. By seven, the kitchen was already reset for the day. Counters wiped, purse and keys lined up, travel mug ready. The clock on the stove hit 7:05, and I nodded to myself. Early, just how I liked it.

"Mom, where are my cleats?" Collin shouted from the hallway.

"By the front door where you left them," I said without looking up.

He grabbed them and bolted out the door. The sound of his sneakers faded down the walkway. It was the sound of a life that worked.

Everything was in order, yet some small part of me didn't trust it. It was near perfect. I didn't know how to live inside of that.

The drive to work was smooth, and my mind ticked through the day ahead like a checklist. Meetings, budgets, staff updates, grocery run, dinner. Days I used to dream about when I was younger, when everything fit inside clean boxes. I parked in my usual spot and walked into the building, heels striking an even cadence. Predictability had become my definition of success.

By mid-morning, the office was moving at its normal pace, nothing amiss. Then my phone buzzed. "Home" flashed on the screen. My parents still had a landline, but my mother's voice was always the first one on the other end.

"Your father's talking nonsense again," she said before I could speak. "He's sitting in that chair saying these people out here just take and take. I told him to stop, but he just keeps talking. He said he was in remission and didn't need his pills."

"Put him on the phone," I said, already knowing she would.

I heard the muffled sound of her handing it off, the little bump of the receiver. Then his voice, faint and wandering.

"Hey, Tahn."

"Hey, Dad. How's things goin'?"

"Eh, everything's alright, but these guys out here, they just take. They take what isn't theirs. You try to do right, and they still take."

"Who's taking what, Dad?"

"You know, the doctors, the politicians, everybody. That's what they do. You can't trust them."

"Okay," I said, keeping my voice steady. "How ya feeling? You alright?"

"I'm fine. Just tired of all this taking. But I'm alright."

He said it like he meant it, but I could hear the strain under his words. The slightest hesitation between sentences. It was a small delay that didn't used to be there.

"Alright," I said again. "I'll call you later."

"Okay," he said, distracted. "Tell Colly Wally I said hi. Bye."

The line dropped. I stared at the phone in my hand long after the call ended. There was some sense of normalcy to it, but something wasn't lining up.

He probably just needs a medication change. The thought settled me, even if I couldn't shake that underlying feeling. I'd call Mom later and see if she could get him to the doctor, then take it from there.

The rest of the day dissolved into movement. Meetings, emails, people asking for decisions. I moved through it easily, a professional on autopilot.

That was the thing about control. It didn't stop the world from cracking; it just kept your hands busy while it did.

By evening, the routine had returned. Dinner on the table. Dishes rinsed. The familiar exchange of words with my husband. He smiled the same easy smile that had once comforted me and now, at times, just filled space. His calm had always balanced me, but lately it felt like silence wearing a mask. I told him about my day. He nodded, half listening.

After we cleaned the kitchen, I made my rounds through the house, turning off lights, locking each door in the same order every night. It wasn't fear. It was habit. Another ritual to remind myself that everything I loved was safe and contained. Upstairs, Collin was finishing homework, and the dogs stretched across the rug beside him. I stood in the hallway and listened. Nothing moved.

That stillness used to feel like victory. Why didn't it anymore?

When Darius and I got into bed, the room went dark except for the soft glow of the clock.

"I feel like something's up," I said quietly.

He murmured a low "uh-huh," already drifting.

Silence filled the space between us.

I turned on my side and stared at the outline of the door. Every part of my life was in order. My job was secure. My marriage peaceful. My children thriving. My parents managing. Everything exactly as I'd hoped for.

So, what? What was this?

I closed my eyes and told myself not to overthink it. Tomorrow would be the same as today. Predictable, calm, and controlled.

But my mind kept cataloging every sound, trying to strategize what could happen next. That call had sharpened something in me. I tried to let it go, but a part of me knew I should prepare. Still, I wanted normalcy. Patterns. The illusion that life could stay the same.

As my eyes grew heavier and the house slipped deeper into its own quiet, my mind finally released its grip.

And for the next few hours, my world stayed like that. Peaceful and certain.

Chapter 8

Descent

I woke up off. Not sick. Not tired. Just off. That phone call still lodged in my chest. My father's voice, the hesitation between his words, the strain underneath. Something wasn't right. I'd told myself it was just a medication adjustment, but my body wasn't buying it. It knew something my mind hadn't caught up to yet.

I couldn't name it. It was just a feeling that wouldn't settle. The unease from the night before hadn't lifted with sleep. If anything, it had deepened.

I had felt this before. Three years earlier, in 2014, when a storm hit my hometown downstate.

The storm itself wasn't memorable. Branches scattered across curbs, traffic crawling through detours. Just another day of bad weather, most people shrugged off. But the storm wasn't it, not fully.

The day after, my father had a dentist appointment.

And that day, he never made it there.

He got lost. In the same town we'd lived in for more than thirty years.

When he finally made it home, he set his keys on the counter and never drove again.

I imagined the fear he must have felt. Circling streets that should have felt familiar or sense landmarks become meaningless. I felt it all unfold in my mother's voice, measured but thin around the edges, when she told me what happened.

"He was just off," she said. "It scared him. Scared me too."

She chalked it up to his schizophrenia. Of course she did. So did my sister. That was the language we knew. If he was different, it had to be an episode. That's how we made sense of the unpredictable, by labeling it. Only this time, the label didn't fit.

He wasn't combative. He wasn't angry. He was confused. Slower. Dimmer in a way that didn't feel like peace.

But we didn't have words for what was happening. We called it stress. A bad day. Maybe he'd forgotten his medication. But something in me started to wonder. The word I kept pushing away was dementia. He was only seventy. That was too young. I told myself it was something else.

In the months that followed, after he had stopped driving, small things began to pile up. He repeated stories. Misplaced simple items.

My mother started handling more of the daily details, but that wasn't new; *she's always done that*, I told myself. Still, there was a difference now, something beneath the surface that none of us could name.

Life moved forward, as it always does.

My parents found their pace again, and I wanted to believe the worst had passed.

But there were hints, small ones at first. Missed calls. Odd comments from my mother that I brushed off as worry. Nothing loud enough to sound the alarm, just that feeling in my chest— the one that tightens before something breaks.

Then Easter Sunday arrived, bright, ordinary, unsuspecting. I opened the windows to let the air in. The sun was warm but not heavy, and the breeze carried that faint sweetness of early spring. Grass, tulips, the promise of something new.

Darius and I moved through the house in sync, getting ready for church. The iron hissed across the fabric. Shoes lined up by the door. The sound of the coffee maker sputtered through its last drip.

I remember thinking how easy the morning felt on our drive to church, how grateful I was for the normalcy. The sun skimmed across the windshield, the windows down just enough for that scent of spring.

My phone rang, and I saw my mother's name on the screen.

I could feel the grip in my chest before I even answered.

"Your father," she said, her voice frantic and tight, "he's talking nonsense. He says he's in *remission* from his diabetes. He hasn't been taking his medication. And now he's yelling at me and accusing me of—things."

That word—*things*—hung in the air. Vague. Off.

I sat up straighter in the car. My body snapped into high alert.

"Put him on the phone," I said.

He got on. His voice was rushed and ragged. His words jumbled full, disconnected thoughts. He kept talking about my mother, but none of it made sense.

"She's . . . talking about things," he said, and I could hear the confusion in his tone. It wasn't anger. It wasn't even agitation. It was something else, something deeper. A fracture.

I hung up and turned to my husband. "We have to go," I said. "It's happening again."

We drove straight downstate.

When we walked through my parents' front door, the scent hit me before anything else. Urine, stale breath, the thick haze of days unshowered.

I found him in the living room, half-dressed, half-dazed. A white tank top on. One sock. One of my mother's slippers on the other foot. His robe hanging off one shoulder.

He looked up and smiled. Reached into his robe pocket and handed me a crumpled twenty-dollar bill.

That was the moment I knew we weren't just in a mental health emergency.

This was physical, too.

We rushed him to the hospital. His kidneys were failing. His blood work was catastrophic. And all the while, he was still talking, still floating somewhere between lucidity and another world entirely.

He was admitted. First for his body. Then for his mind.

I stayed as long as I could, never leaving his side, battling for him because he couldn't.

I fought for tests. For updates. For doctors to *see* the man behind the charts. I advocated like I always had. But this time, it felt different.

This wasn't just another episode.

This was the beginning of something else entirely.

The CT scans came back. White spots. Brain atrophy. The first whisper of dementia spoken out loud.

Later that year, I found the briefcase.

Inside were scraps of paper, napkins, envelopes, each covered in his handwriting. Some pages had dates. Some didn't. A few held complete thoughts, others trailed off mid-sentence. It looked like the inside of a mind trying to hold on to itself.

He never used a cell phone. Never searched symptoms online. He trusted books, the library, the wisdom of printed pages. He was trying to figure out what was happening on his own. Maybe he thought it was another breakdown. Or maybe he knew it wasn't.

He never said a word about it. He just kept reading. Kept writing. Kept trying to solve a puzzle that was already changing shape.

We didn't know then what it would mean. How long would it take? What kind of terrain would we be forced to cross? But something shifted in me that day. A bone-deep knowing that I would keep fighting for him.

I had fought for his rights before. But nothing had prepared me for what it meant to fight for his *mind*.

Chapter 9

Blue and Red

In the months and years that followed my mother's frantic call that Easter morning, life began to change. I left the safety of corporate life and the steadiness of a nine-to-five to build something of my own. Despite my need for routine, I had always carried that entrepreneurial spark, the pull to lead and help others rise into their own power. I wanted to take everything I knew about leadership and pour it into something that mattered.

For a while, it felt like everything was opening up. My world was expanding. I was building, growing, finding a rhythm again.

But as my world stretched wider, my father's began to shrink.

When we talked on the phone, his voice sounded slower. Pauses lingered too long. He'd lose his train of thought mid-sentence, then laugh to smooth over the silence.

Despite those first whispers of dementia on Easter Sunday, I kept telling myself it was nothing, just age creeping in. But that excuse started to sound thin, even to me.

Doctors kept circling through possibilities: dementia, diabetes complications, another turn in the long, unpredictable road of bipolar schizophrenia. None of it felt like an answer. Just words trying to label the delicate threads of my father's health, slowly but surely unraveling.

No one saw my father like I did. Not the illness—the man. He was the caretaker. The one who woke before sunrise, stirring his instant coffee, and always made it home by 3:30 to nap on the couch, the evening news in the background. And I saw that man slipping away, no answers in sight.

My mother would call, her voice stretched tight. "Your dad isn't right today." Some days, I picked up the phone, asked questions, made calls, and tried to troubleshoot from a distance. Some days I couldn't. We were all carrying too much already. I didn't want to go back to the brink again.

But love doesn't loosen its grip just because you're tired.

As I closed out my day, wrapping up client notes from my last session, I shut down for the night. Outside, rain pressed softly against the windows. The cold winter air didn't bother me; warmth drifted from the vent above my bed, brushing across my face as I poured a glass of Pinot Grigio.

I slipped into my favorite pajamas and sat on the edge of the bed, the glass cool in my hand. My body was tired, but it was the good kind of tired. The kind that follows a full day of doing what you love.

I had four clients the next day. I needed sleep.

I reached for my phone to text my sister, curious about how my father was. She had visited him earlier in the day because my mother had gone away to a friend's house for the weekend, leaving him alone. I'd been uneasy about it, but she assured me he'd be fine. She'd left notes taped to the counters, food labeled in the fridge, and his pills set out in careful rows.

I believed her. Or at least I wanted to.

The screen lit up in my hand before I typed a word.

> I went to check on Dad. He seemed okay, but he's acting a little weird.

Weird. The word landed like a crack in glass, small but deep.

I stared at the message, that unease in my chest wrapping itself around each rib and rising. My mother's faith in her systems, her lists, her notes, her schedules, had always held before. This time, though. . . .

I called him. No answer. I tried again. Again, nothing.

Something ancestral rose in me, something instinctual and raw. I yelled for Darius to grab a suitcase, and I started packing. Pajamas. Toiletries. A sweatshirt. I didn't think, I just moved.

The suitcase sat open, waiting—not the little blue one I had packed during my father's first breakdown. I wasn't a child anymore. The luggage was mine now. A red carry-on. One that had rolled behind me into hotel rooms and leadership conferences, into boardrooms and beach vacations. A symbol of movement. Of independence. Of escape. Now it was my armor.

Rain hammered the windshield, the wipers fighting to keep up. The road was empty, just me and the dark. Adrenaline carried me forward. My mind raced with worst-case scenarios—him on the floor, not breathing. Me too late.

When I pulled into the driveway, the house looked undisturbed. I could see light in the living room, but no movement.

I darted up the driveway and opened the front door.

There he was, in the living room, slumped in his recliner, completely still. His Weight Watchers mug lay on the floor, water pooling at his feet.

I thought he was dead.

"Dad," I said, shaking his shoulder. "Can you hear me?"

A small groan, barely there. His lips moved, but the words were jumbled.

I grabbed my phone. "911, what's your emergency?"

"My father," I said. "He's diabetic. He's unconscious but breathing." My voice cracked. "Please hurry. I'm at 103 . . ." I rattled off the address, already unlocking the front door.

"Is he responsive?" the operator asked.

"He was," I said. "Wait—hang on—"

I turned back to him. He stirred, eyelids twitching.

"Dad, stay with me," I begged.

He mumbled something about the bathroom, voice thin and slurred. "Need to go . . . bathroom."

"No," I said. "Stay here. Just stay down, please."

But he tried to stand. His hands fumbled for the armrest, his legs trembling under him. I wrapped one arm around his waist, my other hand still gripping the phone.

"Please," I whispered, "just sit. Please."

But he was already rising. He leaned on me as we stumbled toward the hallway. His weight pressed heavy against mine.

And then he collapsed, almost taking me down with him.

Right there in the bathroom doorway.

"Dad!" I shouted. "Stay with me!"

I held him with one arm, the other fumbling for the phone. "He's down," I said into the air. "Please, just get here."

I couldn't move him.

I tried everything.

I needed him flat. On his back. That was the first thought. Get him on his back. Check his airway. Start CPR if I had to.

But the space was wrong. The half bath too tight. His body angled against the wall, one shoulder wedged, his legs bent in a way I couldn't straighten.

I pulled at him anyway.

Nothing.

I tried again, bracing my feet, shifting my grip, trying to turn him without hurting him.

He didn't move.

Or I couldn't move him.

I don't know which.

My hands slipped. My arms started to shake.

I stopped trying.

Not because I wanted to. Because I had to.

I leaned in close instead, my face near his, watching his chest. Waiting.

Was it moving?

I couldn't tell.

I held him there, one arm across him, the other braced against the wall, like I could keep him from slipping further away.

Time didn't move the way it should. It stretched, then collapsed, then stretched again.

I prayed the only way you pray when words have left you. Not sentences. Not scripture. Just one word, over and over, pushed out of me like breath.

Please.

Please.

Please.

And then, faintly in the distance, I heard the sirens.

The fire department arrived first.

"In here!" I yelled from the doorway. "Hurry!"

They rushed in, voices overlapping, bodies filling the frame. One knelt beside him, checking for a pulse. Another called out vitals. Within seconds, the EMTs were inside too, the hallway filling with the chaos of command.

They moved quickly, practiced. Oxygen levels, blood sugar test. The machine beeped once, then flashed red.

"It maxed out at six hundred," one of them said.

Another radioed ahead. "Call for backup. We need a second unit with a crash cart. We'll meet them on route."

They lifted him onto the stretcher, strapped him down, and rushed toward the door. I followed close behind and grabbed the go bag I'd packed, my hands shaking so badly I could barely zip it. The night air hit like ice as I moved toward the ambulance.

Inside, monitors screamed, and lights flickered across his gray skin. The EMTs worked with urgency, calling out numbers I couldn't make sense of. I watched, frozen and barely breathing, as they tried to keep him alive.

A team stood waiting when we reached the hospital. They slid him onto a new bed, and a new round of procedures began— oxygen, fluids, vitals, blood draw.

A doctor rushed into the room, chart in hand.

"It's nine hundred and three," she said, her voice urgent, almost shouting it to the team.

And the room exploded into motion.

It was life-saving chaos, and all I could do was wait.

He shouldn't have survived. But he did.

The machines quieted. The room emptied. And I was left staring at the man I almost lost.

While he stabilized in the hospital, I watched and drifted beside him, sleeping in the unforgiving hospital chair when I could, curled under thin blankets, listening to the beeps and hums that marked each passing hour. I counted the minutes between nurse checks, memorized the shift rotations, and watched as the color slowly returned to my father's face. I was exhausted in a way no nap could fix. My body ached, but I wouldn't leave.

My mother and sister came once, early on, before the world shut down completely. After that, visitors were turned away at the door. Somehow, I was allowed to stay. I think because the nurses had seen me there from the very first night. I don't know if it was policy or mercy. I didn't ask.

And in the background—always—the news. On the room TV, on my phone, in my ears like a pulse. COVID cases rising. Wards overflowing. Cities beginning to shut down. Each day, new restrictions. Each hour, more fear. I was afraid that if I stepped out, they wouldn't let me back in. So, I stayed—on edge, unshowered, unslept, half-fed, operating on vending machine snacks and coffee that tasted like cardboard. I didn't care. I just needed to be close enough to see him breathe. I was already in survival mode, long before the world realized it would need to be too.

When the doctors started talking about transferring him to a rehab, something inside me clicked. I didn't cry. I didn't panic. I went into problem-solving mode. I called anyone I knew who could help. I searched for contacts. Prayed into voicemails. And then—a miracle. A friend whose daughter worked at a facility called me back. They could get him in.

They moved him from the ICU to a standard room. Then stricter protocols kicked in. Fewer visitors. More rules. Nurses in masks. Hand sanitizer at every door. And slowly, I began to feel myself being shut out. As cases increased, so did the distance between me and the one person I had vowed never to abandon.

I didn't argue, but inside I was panicking.

Who will speak for him when I'm not there?

What if he forgets how to ask for help?

What if he catches the virus and dies alone?

Eventually, they transferred him to the nursing rehab that hadn't yet reported any positive cases. I exhaled briefly. I had my friend's daughter there; that single thread of connection held me together. Her updates were consistent and reassuring. A lifeline of information I knew I never would've received if she hadn't been there.

Still, the forced separation ate away at me and the little sleep I could get.

My father couldn't understand why no one was visiting, why he was trapped inside a place that didn't feel like home. "I can see the road," he said one afternoon on the phone, "but nobody will let me go to it."

I swallowed the lump in my throat, forcing my voice to sound calm. He didn't need to sense my fear on top of his confusion.

"I'll find out why they won't let you and call you back," I said, pretending I could fix it. Pretending there was still something left to fix.

When I hung up, the lie sat heavy in my chest. It wasn't cruel. It wasn't careless. It was mercy in disguise, a soft rewrite of reality that momentarily eased us both. But it was still a lie. And it was to my father, the one person I never wanted to deceive. He trusted me to tell him the truth, and I had broken something sacred between us.

There's a kind of grace in small lies, the kind that keeps a fragile mind from breaking under a truth too heavy to hold. I told myself I did it for him, but part of me knew I was doing it for me. Because if I admitted he was trapped, I'd have to face that I couldn't free him.

That was the first of many small graces—tiny fictions dressed as comfort.

Each one built a small barrier between us, soft enough to feel kind, solid enough to keep me from falling apart. It was also how I learned to gain the compliance I would need and keep him calm in a world that had become foreign to him.

That road. I can still see it.

A metaphor. A warning. A goodbye.

Alone in my hotel room the night before they transferred him to the nursing rehab, I stared at the red suitcase. Propped open. Half-packed. Half-prepared.

That suitcase had once been a lifeline to my freedom.

Now, it was my witness.

It held my toothbrush and the clothes I'd bought at a nearby Walmart because I hadn't prepared for all this—not the world on pause or my father's almost passing. It also held my fear. My fatigue. My silent prayers. The kind you whisper into the air and hope someone or something is listening.

Outside, the air felt heavy with something unnamed. I didn't yet realize how much my life was about to change; I only knew I was standing at the edge of a world unraveling by the hour.

I could feel the girl I had been, the one who had packed her bag all those years ago to flee her father's madness. Now I was a grown woman determined to stay, my bag at the ready—determined to save him from a failing body in a broken system.

I told myself things would stabilize, that this was temporary, that normal would return.

But there were no manuals for caregiving in a global pandemic.

Believe me, I looked. I searched for anything that might tell me how to keep him safe when I couldn't be at his side. How to advocate for him from a distance. How to sleep at night knowing a virus could slip through the hallway and take him before I said goodbye.

All I had were my instincts. Gut reactions. The reserves of strength I hoped I hadn't lost beneath the layers of fatigue and fear, buried under the weight of responsibility I never asked for but carried anyway.

Chapter 10

The Night Before

I knew my father could no longer return to the life he had. The dementia had reached a point where my mother could no longer manage it. And I knew, too, that soon he would need to live with me. That I would have to make space, not just in my home but in every corner of my life.

I remember the date he moved in like a scar that never fades: April 16, 2020. But the night before—before the move, before the monitors and pills and alarms—my body felt the weight of what my mind was still resisting. That life as I knew it was going to change.

Still, like always, my strong side said I could handle it.

The night before, I sat down in the living room of my parents' home, my old home. The furniture in the same place it had been since the 90s. The house was dim and quiet. My mother scuffled around in the kitchen, pouring herself a glass of wine. Next to me on the couch sat Marlene. Our friendship went back decades. She came into my life through a family who had followed mine from Yonkers to Beacon back in '76.

We danced in the same clubs, closed them down some nights, bought houses on the same street where I grew up years later.

Through marriages, kids, everything that came and went, she was just always there.

"You know this is gonna be tough," Marlene said gently, folding her hands around her glass of wine. "You have to pace yourself." She had worked as a CNA and carried the grounded kind of wisdom that comes from witnessing the unfixable. "He's going to decline. It's going to be hard sometimes. You sure you can do this?"

"I know," I said, even though I didn't. I was already half gone into planning mode. What room would he sleep in? Which doctors did I need? What meds? What lists? The things that made me feel like I could still control what was coming.

From the kitchen, my mother spoke up. "Why do they think he can't come here?" Her tone was clipped, part guilt, part denial.

We all knew the truth. My father could no longer live with her. His confusion had deepened; her patience had not. Saying it out loud in that living room, under the soft glow of the old lamp, didn't feel like betrayal. It felt like a necessity. She wasn't equipped for what was coming, no matter how much she believed she could be.

Marlene took a slow sip of her wine and shook her head. "I still can't believe you found him like that. Good thing you came down. What happened?"

I looked down at my glass of wine. "He was in his chair when I got here. Completely still. His mug was on the floor. . . water everywhere. I thought—" I stopped. "I thought he was gone."

Marlene exhaled, her hand pressing briefly to her chest. "God."

She shook her head again. "Your dad was everybody's person. He'd see you walking down the street, 'hi, how ya doin', always the neighborhood nurse."

I smiled. "Yeah, remember his truck?"

She laughed. "Yup, the wood deliveries. He'd have half the street talking when that truck showed up. Out there all day cutting, stacking, carrying it all around back like he was building an empire."

"Every single year," I said, shaking my head. "'Gotta chop the wood,' he'd say."

"He is one of the good ones, you know. The kind you don't forget."

"I know."

Then she grinned. "Just promise me, if he tries to give you a tomato. . . . Remember the cookout when your mother gave him one to bring down to my house?"

"How are you gonna bring one tomato to a cookout?"

We both cracked up, remembering. Our laughter filling every corner of the house.

From the kitchen, my mother's voice cut through. "Are you two drunk?"

"Maybe," Marlene called back. "So are you!"

For a second, even my mother smirked. The tension dropped just enough for us to breathe.

Marlene reached over and squeezed my hand. "I know you; you got this. You always do."

"I will," I said, and meant it. "He'll be okay with me. I can manage the day-to-day. It's too much for her."

We stayed on the couch a while longer, the mood softer now, both of us nursing what was left in our glasses. Our conversation drifted into that easy back and forth only old friends have, half laughter and half memory, catching up on each other's lives, musing over how strange it felt to live in a world where grocery stores had no toilet paper, and everyone kept six feet apart.

My phone buzzed against the coffee table, my daughter's name on the screen.

"It's Bri," I said, smiling as I reached for it. I figured she was calling to ask about her grandfather or when I'd be heading back upstate. I answered quickly.

"Hey Bri, how ya doin?"

Her breath trembled through the line. "Mom. . . ."

Something in her tone made my heart pause. "What's up? You okay?"

"He's gone."

The words didn't land right away. "What?"

"My father," she said. "He came home this morning, but he's gone. They said it was peaceful." I could hear the tears in her voice.

The air left the room. Marlene turned toward me, eyes wide, trying to read what I'd just heard.

"He was just sent home," I whispered, mostly to myself.

Brianna and Collin's father had been gone long before he died. His body was the last thing that left. I raised my children mostly on my own, with the help of my parents, filling the spaces his absence created. I felt the deep ache of watching her lose the idea of him all over again.

"They said a few days," I said, still in shock. The room felt tilted. My father arriving tomorrow. Her father gone today. The same night, holding both.

"Yeah," Bri said. Her voice cracked. "I thought I'd have time to say goodbye."

I pressed my hand over my eyes, trying to hold myself together. "I'm so sorry," I said, my voice catching. It wasn't grief for him that broke me. It was hearing my daughter's heart crack on the other end of the line.

Marlene watched me, unsure what to say. The house around us felt heavier, the air thick with too much grief. Two men, too many ways to lose them.

It was strange how loss could move that fast. How one life could leave in the morning and be gone by nightfall. Outside, headlines grieved the thousands dying each day, bodies without funerals, goodbyes without touch.

Now grief had landed in my own living room.

I tried to stay calm for her, though my throat ached. "I'm here," I told her softly. "You're not alone. We'll get through this."

After she hung up, I sat there for a long time, the phone still in my hand.

Marlene finally spoke. "I'm so sorry," she said. "I feel bad for her. What happened?"

I nodded, staring at nothing. "He came home earlier this morning on hospice," I said, my voice landing flat. "They said days."

She looked at me, startled. "That fast?" she whispered, shocked.

I nodded. "That fast."

For a while, neither of us said anything. My glass sat untouched on the table. Outside, the rain had started again, soft against the window.

It hit me then how fragile everything had become. Life, plans, even time itself. One man had come home to die that morning, another would come home to live the next day. Both journeys pulling us into something we could never undo.

I didn't know it yet, but that night was a rehearsal for what was coming. Loss after loss—some of them sudden, some of them gradual, all of them out of my control. Already, they were circling, dark and graceful teachers of how to hold on and how to let go at the same time.

Chapter 11

The Ride Home

Not long after I moved out of my childhood home, Dad had taken over my old room and made it his own. But traces of me were still tucked into the space. The gray carpet I chose. The border I hung myself. That room had once been the first place I claimed as mine. My private kingdom. New carpet. Fresh paint. A lock on the door. A phone line of my own.

It was never rebellion. It was autonomy. It was control. A place where I could breathe without interruption and where my voice belonged only to me.

When I moved out, he quietly turned the space into his own sanctuary. His books. His papers. His thoughts spread everywhere. It still smelled faintly of his aftershave and newspaper ink. He used to read constantly. Philosophy. Psychology. Ancient history. Books stacked up wherever he sat. At the time it felt like a quirk. Only later did I understand it as his way of steadying himself against a storm he could feel forming inside his mind.

The morning of April 16, I stood at the window with my coffee and watched the light cut across the driveway. I knew my life was about to shift. No more planning. No more weighing options. Today, my father was coming home with me for good.

When I arrived at the rehab facility, the reality of the world mirrored back the strangeness plastered across headlines. A sign taped to the glass read **NO VISITORS BEYOND THIS POINT**. Inside the vestibule, every surface carried an instruction. Wear a mask. Sanitize your hands. Keep your distance. On a narrow shelf sat sanitizer bottles and an intercom button.

I pressed it.

"Name and relation?"

"I am here for William Robinson. I am his daughter, Tahnya, here for his discharge."

"Please wait in the vestibule."

The inner door buzzed open into an abandoned lobby. Chairs were stacked against the wall. Old decorations sagged on a bulletin board like a season that never finished.

Then I saw him.

A nurse in full PPE pushed his wheelchair. Another followed with a clear plastic bag. Pajama bottoms. A fleece. One slipper. That was everything he had left in that place.

His eyes landed on me and lit up. His whole face opened. Pure, startled joy after weeks surrounded by strangers behind shields.

"Hey, Tahn," he said, voice soft but bright.

"Hey, Dad. You ready to get out of here?"

He nodded quickly. "Been ready."

The nurse rolled him toward the door and paused so I could take over. I placed my hand on his shoulder through the thin bathrobe. He looked up at me like that touch was proof we had survived something together.

As I reached for the wheelchair brakes, I felt the shift inside me.

I was on.

He was being discharged with a catheter and a stack of vague papers. What awaited us was a maze of appointments, insurance updates, new doctors, and legal decisions. A whole system I would now have to manage on his behalf.

But he did not need that truth.

Not today.

Not when he could barely separate one memory from another.

So, I created a story he could accept.

I didn't tell him the facility was on lockdown. I said, "We're going home for a bit."

Caregivers learn that not every truth is helpful. There is a term for it. Therapeutic fibbing. It sounds official, like something invented by someone who has never actually cared for a confused parent, but caregivers know it is actually survival. It is choosing peace instead of panic. It is choosing comfort instead of fear.

You don't correct them when they ask for people who are no longer here. You answer with warmth instead of history. It is survival. It is protection.

And with my father, a registered nurse who spent his entire career in a men's prison and who had a long, complicated mistrust of doctors, I could not yet use the word "doctor."

"Where are we going?" he asked.

"Just a few errands," I said calmly. "Then lunch at my house. The dogs will be excited to see you."

His shoulders softened. "Yeah. Lunch sounds good."

Outside, the air felt clean and cool. I helped him into the passenger seat, buckled him in, and tucked a blanket across his lap. I sprayed sanitizer into his hands.

"What do I do with this?"

"Just rub your hands together. There is a pandemic, so we are keeping things clean."

Halfway through the drive, he looked down and noticed the catheter bag.

"What is this doing here?"

"That is why we are stopping by the doctor," I said gently. "Just a quick look. It's one of our errands."

He frowned, then nodded. "Okay. If it's quick."

At discharge, no one had explained a single detail about the catheter. Not the schedule. Not the signs of infection. Not how often it needed to be emptied. They handed me a plastic bag and paperwork printed in tiny letters.

"Can someone show me how to manage this?" I had asked the nurse.

She glanced at the clock. "Urology will cover that when you get there."

In other words, not my problem.

"No," I said. Steady. Clear. "I need the basics now."

She blinked, surprised that I pushed. She left the vestibule. Five minutes later, another nurse came in. Kinder. More patient. She walked me through everything and wrote her extension on the discharge sheet.

"You'll be fine," she said. "I checked everything myself. The tubing. The tape. The placement. Just make sure he doesn't pull on it."

These are the things no one tells you unless you push. You get sent out into a parking lot with a catheter and a loved one, and you are expected to figure it out as you go.

That is caregiving.

You don't receive training.

You receive a person you love.

And then you learn.

I knew in that moment: This was my life now. My job. Not just as his daughter, but as his advocate. His caregiver.

The truth is that I had been preparing for this for years. Decades, really.

When I was nineteen, my mother called with panic in her voice. "Something happened with your father today at work. They treated him horribly. He is not okay." My father had been humiliated publicly by his supervisor. Not for incompetence. For being different. For thinking differently. For slipping through the cracks in ways he did not yet have language for.

That was the first time I understood what I would do for him. I didn't have a degree or connections. I had my voice. So I wrote letters. I made calls. I pushed past every excuse. And when I needed to, I called back as Ms. Robinson from the Office of Patient Advocacy because that version of me got answers.

So, when it came to navigating a system that exhausted people like my father, I knew I was the right person for the job. I always had been.

We arrived at the urologist's office and got my father inside.

"What are we doing here?" he asked several times while we waited for the doctor to enter.

I would answer with the truth—"just waiting for the doctor"— then start some meaningless conversation about the family to distract him. But eventually the question came again.

"What are we doing here, Tahn?"

"Just waiting for the doctor to tell you about that bag. We are going to my house for lunch right after this."

He smiled. "That is good because I am hungry. These people don't feed you here."

With that agreement, I exhaled. Relief came in small doses that I would later see as gifts.

On the drive upstate after the appointment, I played Ray Charles. My father leaned back in his seat and listened.

The first time I remember hearing Ray was in Dad's old blue Chevy pickup. The window was cracked, and the cold air crept in. "Hit the Road Jack" came on the radio. He turned it up to sing along.

"Hit the road, Jack, and don't ya come back no more, no more, no more, no more..." he sang, drumming the steering wheel. "He was one of the greatest, Tahn. Boy, could he sing. Had a lot of women too," he said with a laugh.

Now, decades later, his fingers twitched against the blanket. Almost in rhythm. For a moment, he was himself again. The man who danced in the kitchen at every party, and believed music could fix almost anything. It was as if he remembered himself young and full of life with experiences still ahead of him.

The music anchored us. I waited for the questions I thought would come:

Why is it taking so long?

Why are we not going home?

Which home?

Those questions never came.

Maybe he was relieved. Maybe he was simply free. Maybe being next to someone familiar after weeks of strangers was enough.

As we pulled up to the house, he exclaimed, "This is your house?!"

"Yeah, it is, Dad. We're gonna go inside and see Darius and the dogs and have a great big yummy lunch."

I kept my promise, whether he knew it or not. We sat down to a late lunch and an early dinner, though I don't remember what we ate. I only remember watching him eat and feeling grateful he could.

Later, after a few laughs and an episode of *The Lone Ranger*, I sensed he was tired. He stirred, stood, and began searching for something, or somewhere.

"What's up, Dad? You tired? You ready for bed?"

"Yeah. I gotta go home."

"Follow me." I walked him upstairs. Confusion crossed his face. He knew this was not his room, but something felt familiar. He didn't argue when I handed him his pajamas and helped him change, being careful around the catheter bag. I tucked him in and turned off the light.

"Good night, sleep tight, see you in the morning light," I said.

"Love you," he whispered as he wiggled under the sheets to get comfortable.

Then, miraculously, he went to sleep in his new home.

The home that would become his safety.

The home that would become his prison.

The home where I would one day whisper that it was okay to let go.

That night was the beginning of my caregiving journey.

I had no idea what would come next.

Only that I crossed the threshold with no map.

Only memory.

And love.

Chapter 12

The Fight for Control

The day after my father moved in, I was inundated with a barrage of texts and missed calls asking how things were going since my ex-husband passed. The notifications stacked on my phone faster than I could clear them. Friends I hadn't spoken to in years. People who meant well. People who wanted information I didn't have. One of his closest friends called to check on us, especially my daughter. Others asked about arrangements, about services, about what came next, as if there were answers already lined up.

We were in New York. He had been living in South Carolina. He had remarried. That was the extent of what I really knew about his life. Honestly, I wasn't thinking about arrangements. I was thinking about survival.

I stood at the living room bay window with my coffee, warming my hands, watching a flock of geese cut through our yard. Everything seemed to be changing at once, right in front of me, and I couldn't tell yet which changes mattered most.

I texted Bri:

> How you holdin up?

> I'll be OK, she responded. They can't do anything for him in terms of a service, so I am not sure what is next.

> If you want to come by later and see grandpa, you can. We are all OK, nobody is sick here.

> Yeah, I'll see,

> I think I just want to be alone.

She was trying to hold it together before the reality of it fully landed. She posted on Facebook, and the condolences poured in. She wouldn't get to say goodbye. Funerals were postponed. Services were canceled. Loss had become private, witnessed through screens instead of pews and funeral homes.

I took a sip of coffee when I heard movement upstairs. A drawer opening. Closing. Opening again.

I set my phone down and headed toward the stairs.

The hallway smelled faintly of laundry detergent and dryer sheets from my husband's most recent batch. He was trying to make sure my father had some clothes to wear since he came home with nothing besides some socks, a pair of jeans, and pajamas.

"I washed these for him," Darius said, handing me the small pile. "I also have some stuff that may fit him. I will take a look in a minute."

"Thanks," I said. "I can't believe they lost all of his clothes. For Christ's sake, we put his name on EVERYTHING!" I shook my head, unable to comprehend all the small ways my father had already been failed by a system supposed to help. "But at least he's home and away from all the COVID spiraling through the nursing homes and hospitals. He got out by the skin of his teeth."

"You got that right. I'll make up his bed and find those clothes once I am done with this laundry."

"Sounds good, thanks."

I walked up the stairs to the third floor, knocked lightly on my father's door, and pushed it open. He was standing at the dresser, pulling drawers open and shut, his face riddled with frustration.

"Morning, Dad. How did you sleep?"

"I slept good," he said, not turning around. "But I can't find my—"

"Are you looking for clothes to get changed?"

He nodded. "Yeah. Can you help me?"

"Sure. I got you. Darius is washing some of your things right now."

I pulled out the only pair of jeans we had and gave him one of Darius' sweaters, and then helped him into the bathroom.

"Why is this here?" he asked, pointing at the catheter bag.

"You were in the hospital," I said gently. "You had trouble with your kidneys. They had to put it in. You know what it is. You were a nurse."

"I don't need it now."

"We'll see the doctor in a few days," I said. "They'll take care of it."

He sighed. "Alright. But they better take it out."

"I'm sure they will."

Downstairs, I had already made his breakfast. Coffee with half-and-half. Two packets of Sweet 'N Low. Applesauce. Raisin Bran.

His staples.

"Wow," he said, looking at the table. "Is that all for me?"

"Breakfast fit for a king," offering him a seat at the head of the table.

He smiled and ate quietly, staring out the back door toward the woods. Everything felt almost normal.

And that was what made it so disorienting.

I watched him closely as he spooned cereal into his mouth, and I waited for him to look up and ask where he was, or why he was there, or when my mother was coming to get him.

I had kept our landline, just in case. Next to it, I'd written phone numbers on a whiteboard in thick black marker. My mother's. Mine. My husband's. My daughter's. And 911, written larger than the rest, labeled **EMERGENCY**. Just in case.

I wasn't fully aware yet of what he could or couldn't do. I didn't know what he understood or what he remembered. He looked the same. Thin now. A little frail from everything he'd been through. But still my dad. The smart guy who loved to read.

The man who always had an opinion about whatever was happening in the world.

I expected him to ask for a newspaper. But that request never came. Instead, when I asked if he wanted to watch some TV, he answered with an energetic, almost boyish, "Yeah, cmon let's go."

We went down into the family room, put on a movie, and let the day pass by. I sat there beside him, half-watching the screen, half-watching his face, aware of how much vigilance it took to protect something that looked so peaceful—and how quietly, without warning, that peace could vanish.

Later that night, after the house finally went quiet, he was in bed in clean, comfortable pajamas. I sat down at the desk in my office, laptop open, the glow from the screen the only light on. I told myself I was just going to look up one thing.

There was this internal nudge I couldn't ignore. I needed to know. I needed to understand what could happen. I kept replaying the conversation with Marlene—her gentle but pressing concern, her advice to pace myself—and the catheter situation was still sitting heavy with me. Unresolved and unsettling.

I started scrolling.

One article turned into ten. Tabs stacked across the top of my browser until I couldn't see the titles anymore. Alzheimer's stages. Dementia timelines. Caregiver forums. Medical journals written in language I had to reread three times just to grasp the basics.

I clung to the desperate hope that knowledge could equal

control. If I could just understand this disease enough, I could get ahead of it. Predict it. Manage it.

This is bullshit, I thought, exhausted from searching.

Why in the ever-loving hell isn't there one place with clear answers? One road map? One guide for what comes next?

The frustration kept mounting until it stopped feeling like research and started feeling like a game I was losing, and badly. Like being down 0-44 in the second half, knowing no one was coming off the bench to save you. The clock on my screen stared back at me as it crept past 12:30 a.m. I had an early morning. I took the loss and told myself I'd figure it out when I was rested.

Morning came fast.

Chirp. Chirp. Chirp.

My alarm sounded at its ever-familiar 6:00 a.m. Time to make his breakfast.

Coffee. Half-and-half. Sweet 'N Low. Raisin Bran. Yogurt this time, not applesauce. He needed variety.

Same process. Different day.

I got him dressed. Buttoned the shirt. Straightened the collar. Shoes on. Socks matched. We went downstairs, and he ate in peace while I made my own coffee and talked out loud, narrating the morning as if the words themselves could keep everything in place.

All the while, a checklist played on repeat in my mind:

We'll plant a garden. That will keep his mind busy.

We'll take walks.

Play with the dogs.

Puzzles. Yes, puzzles will help.

I repeated it as if, said clearly enough, in the right order, it would hold.

But what no one told me—what I couldn't find after hours and hours of searching, reading, scouring the internet for answers— is that caring for someone with dementia is like trying to corral a storm with your bare hands.

I wasn't caring for a toddler I could scoop up and carry back inside when he refused to listen.

I was caring for a six-foot-tall, seventy-six-year-old man who weighed one hundred and eighty-five pounds.

And when he didn't want to do something? He just wouldn't do it.

"How was breakfast, Dad?"

"It was great, thanks. What now, Tahn?"

"Well, I have some work to do. Do you want to go watch some TV while I go upstairs for one of my meetings?"

"Yeah, let's go," he said, already standing.

We walked into the living room and, to my immediate relief, *Gunsmoke* was on Tubi.

"You good, you cold? Do you need a blanket?"

"Nah, I'm alright. What are these fellas doing?" he asked, pointing at the dogs like they were uninvited guests.

"That's Lola and Creed. They wanna watch TV with you."

"OK, I guess. Turn it up a little."

"Here's some water for ya, and I will be right upstairs if you need me. Just come around the corner, up the stairs, and come get me. Okay?"

"Yup," he replied, half listening to me and totally engulfed in the show.

I snuck upstairs to my office, leaving the door open so I could hear if he needed me. Then I hopped on my Zoom call and started my day. I wrapped up my meetings and went down to make my father lunch. The process was becoming just that, a routine, repeatable, and simple. Eat. Nap. Watch TV.

That little window of time was my chance to catch up on emails, exhale for a moment, and convince myself I was still balancing caregiving with my actual life.

I got him settled with a peanut butter and jelly sandwich and a Diet Coke, then went back to my desk to get some work done. I was fully focused and in control. Too focused, though. When I looked at the clock again, I had been working for 30 minutes straight, forgetting Dad was downstairs finishing up lunch.

Fuck! I thought. *I hope he figured out how to go back to the living room to finish his show.* But something felt off. My gut pushed me to get down there, and fast.

I couldn't find him in the family room.

Or the kitchen.

I checked the formal living room next, and it was empty.

"Dad?" I called.

Nothing.

My heart started pounding.

I checked the bathroom. Empty.

I ran back into the family room, my eyes darting to the TV—the Western was still playing. The same show. The same scene. As if nothing had changed.

But something had changed.

I turned toward the front door—and my stomach dropped.

It was wide open.

I hadn't known this was something I needed to prepare for.

How did none of those articles mention this?

I didn't know then that *wandering* was part of the disease.

But I knew it now. And I knew what could happen next.

I knew what happened when elderly people with dementia walked into traffic.

I knew what happened when the police picked them up, mistaking confusion for aggression.

My mind went there, to the horror stories I'd read. To the headlines about men like my father being tackled, detained, and treated like criminals because they had lost their way.

And then, the worst thought hit me.

People are going to think I can't take care of him.

I was his caregiver. His daughter. And I had lost him.

And we were still in a pandemic—no help was coming.

I ran outside, scanning both ends of the street.

Nothing.

I sprinted back inside, grabbed my car keys, and called 911 as I threw the car into drive.

I could barely get the words out.

"My father—he has dementia—he's missing—he was just here—I don't know where he is."

The dispatcher's voice was calm, steady. Asking me what he was wearing and where I had last seen him.

Last seen him?

I didn't even have an answer. He had just been there.

I drove wildly through the neighborhood, scanning every sidewalk, every driveway. The streets were too empty, my mind too full:

What if he walked into the road?

What if someone called the cops on him?

What if someone hurt him?

What if I never see him again?

"Stay on the line," the dispatcher told me, but my breathing was ragged, my hands white-knuckling the steering wheel.

Then, suddenly, her voice changed.

"Someone just called in about a man standing on their property, looking confused."

She gave me the street name, and I flew there.

As I turned the corner, my stomach clenched.

There he was. Sweatshirt draped over his arm, water jug in hand, standing under a tree—a mile and a half from home.

The police arrived just as I did. I jumped out of the car, breathless, shaking.

"Dad, what are you doing? Where were you going?"

He just smiled, that signature Fast Eddie grin.

"I was going home, but I couldn't find the house. Can you help me?"

I swallowed the lump in my throat. Held back the tears burning behind my eyes.

"Yeah, Dad. I'll help you."

I got him in the car and drove home, shaken to my core.

No one had told me that wandering was part of this disease.

I had no idea that life was about to become a never-ending game of staying one step ahead of his mind.

I had no idea that control—the thing I had always relied on to keep that illusion of safety close—was about to slip completely from my grasp.

I texted my best friend, Ninette, my hands still shaking:

Holy FUCK, my dad got out of the house and walked over a mile away before I could find him.

Wait what?

What happened?

I was in my office working, and he must have decided it was a nice day for a walk, WTF? I was petrified.

Oh God, is he OK?

Yeah. But I don't know if I am. TTYL.

I put my phone down and just stood there, rattled. I couldn't believe I had let that happen.

What did I do wrong? I kept asking myself over and over. What did I miss? It was only thirty minutes.

Thirty minutes!

This can't happen again.

No, I wouldn't let it, I decided. Once was enough.

So, I sprang into action. Work was officially over for the day. After that ordeal, I couldn't wrap my mind around project scopes and business strategies. This was now my only focus. I got him upstairs for a well-deserved nap, and I started building systems the way people do in movies, convinced that if I added enough locks, enough safeguards, enough rules, nothing could get out.

I called the security company and scheduled an appointment to have cameras installed everywhere. The house wasn't built for this. We'd designed it for family gatherings. For laughter. For people spilling onto couches and into corners of rooms. Its levels and long sight lines made it feel open and inviting; now it made me nervous.

I needed every door fitted with a chime. Every floor installed with eyes and ears. Every window accounted for. I searched frantically online for child safety locks and came up empty. Nothing was designed for a grown man who wanted to go home, who was confused but still capable. He knew how to open a lock. He was fast. This was me against a mind that kept changing the rules.

Later that night, after Darius got home, I told him what had happened. I explained how slick Dad had been. How fast. How stealthy. How I'd found him over a mile away, standing under a tree like he'd been waiting for someone to recognize him and tell him where he belonged.

"Going forward," I said, "we have to be relentless. Locking things up can't be occasional anymore. It has to be constant. Day and night. This isn't temporary. This is the new system."

He nodded, taking it in.

"I have the security company coming tomorrow to install cameras," I continued. "The locksmith will be here around noon. I'm not going to work. The team will handle things. They know what's going on."

"Okay," he said. "Do you want me to stay home?"

I shook my head. "No. I don't want you taking days off, especially since you just got back to work."

"Is there anything else I can do?"

The question hung there between us.

I looked at him. Really looked at him. Trying to find a way to say what I actually needed instead of what was easy to ask for.

There was more I wanted to express. About how fast it had happened. About how quiet Dad had been when he slipped out. About how I couldn't shake the feeling that the house itself, this house we'd chosen, this house I'd designed to feel safe, was now working against me. About how scared I still was. About how this already felt like something I was doing alone, even though he was standing right here.

I wanted to say: *I need you to see me. To really see me. Not just hear the logistics, but understand that I'm drowning.*

Instead, I heard myself say, "No. I've got it."

"Alright," he said. "Sounds good."

He said it the way he always did. Easy. Agreeable. Like the words landed cleanly, and the conversation was complete. Like information exchanged meant connection made. Like checking a box was the same thing as being present.

I stood there a second longer, waiting.

Waiting for a follow-up question. For him to lean in instead of pulling back. For him to stay in it with me instead of moving on. For him to ask *how are you holding up,* or *what do you need from me,* or *this sounds really hard,* or anything that acknowledged the weight of what I was carrying.

We were in it—the part no one warns you about. The unspoken expectation that your partner will *see* you. That they'll hear what you're saying and what you can't quite articulate yet. That they won't make you spell it out or ask twice when you're already standing there raw and exhausted and barely holding it together.

But he didn't see it.

Not the panic still sitting in my chest from finding Dad in the middle of the street.

Not the exhaustion of knowing this was just the beginning.

Not the fear that was threading through every single decision I was making now.

He saw a problem. And problems had solutions. Something we were both good at finding. Something we could both talk about. Cameras. Locks. Systems.

And once the solution was named, he was done.

I felt something harden inside me then. Not anger exactly. Not even surprise.

Just clarity.

Cold. Sharp. Undeniable.

In this part of it—the planning, the watching, the constant vigilance—I'm going to be on my own.

He had heard the information. But he hadn't heard the weight behind it. He hadn't felt what it was costing me to hold all of it at once. The systems, the constant watchfulness. The fear that now sat just under my skin like a second pulse.

I could have tried again. I could have slowed it all down and said, *No, wait. That's not what I meant. I need you to sit with me in this. I need you to feel this with me, not just fix it.*

But I didn't.

Because I already knew how it would end.

With distance.

With frustration.

With me carrying it anyway.

So, I let it go.

He moved into his routine, checking doors, turning off lights, doing the small tasks that made him feel useful. I watched him move through the house like everything was under control now. Like the problem had been solved. Like we could go to bed and tomorrow would be normal again.

We both reached for the lamps on our nightstands and turned them off at the same time, the room dropping into darkness. A routine we knew by heart.

"Goodnight," he said.

"Goodnight," I replied.

I lay there listening to his breathing even out, steady and predictable, the sound of someone who believed the crisis had been handled. Someone who could let it go and sleep.

I stayed awake.

My mind kept replaying the day. The doors. The timing. The moments I'd missed. What I could have done differently. What I'd need to do tomorrow. And the next day. And the day after that.

The house was still around us. Doors closed. Lights off. Systems in place.

It looked safe.

I wasn't.

And somewhere in the space between his steady breathing and my racing thoughts, I understood something I hadn't let myself admit before.

This gap between us wasn't new.

It had been there for a while.

I'd just been too busy to notice it widening.

Chapter 13

Respect the Shoes

I walked toward Dad's room with that small jolt of unease before you open a door. Every day, even after a year of living with us, he still surprised me.

I opened the door and found him in his room already half-dressed in an unseasonably warm outfit for July: Jeans. Long-sleeve shirt. And a sweatshirt.

"It's hot out, Dad," I said, folding the hood back from his neck.

"No, no, no, it isn't," he answered, the way he always did.

I convinced him into a T-shirt; he slipped the hoodie right back on. I tied his shoes and rubbed lotion into the backs of his hands. He watched my hands work, as if this were a ritual we both understood.

"Nice day," he said, like he had ordered the weather himself.

"It is. Let's sit outside for a bit."

I took a cold soda to the deck, then walked him out slow, step by step. The rail was warm under my palm. Fresh-cut grass in the air. Around the corner, Darius coaxed the mower; it coughed, tried again, then caught.

"Collin's gonna come down and maybe go swimming later. You gonna join him?"

He sat, patted his knee, and looked over the yard as if taking attendance. Fence. Maple. Pool.

"Nah, I don't swim, you know that, but the pool looks nice. Nice place!"

"Team effort."

He smiled at that. The old smile. The one that said he still recognized the life we had built, even if he could no longer name every part of it.

We were in a good stretch. He was eating. He was sleeping. He would laugh. I could breathe.

Noon hit, and the planks radiated like a stove-top. My soda sweat through my koozie. Collin came out with a towel over his shoulder and sneakers too clean for this world.

"Gramps, the burgers today are gonna slap," he said.

Dad's eyebrows went up. "Wait now, you can't do a thing like that."

Collin grinned. "No, it's like . . . it's like when, when you have something that's so good, it makes you wanna slap your mama."

Dad shook his head, dead serious. "Now, now, you can't do that. First of all, your other family members would get you, and then your father's going to kick your brains out if he hears about it. Then they got the, the brothers and the sisters, you can't slap your mama. C'mon, Col, can't do stuff like that."

I laughed first. Collin broke right after. Dad tried to hold his expression, then a soft chuckle slipped out, and the whole scene let go.

They talked about shoes next. Shiny. Kept clean. "Had mine so polished you could see yourself," he said.

"Respect the shoes," Collin said.

"That's right. Respect the shoes."

It went like that for hours. What began as a casual deck conversation grew into something deeper. My father—despite the disease, despite his world shrinking—still held pieces of himself: the storyteller, the teacher, the quick-witted man. And Collin, the eager audience, leaned in to learn. In the chaos of caregiving, I almost missed what was forming between them—two men at opposite ends of a bridge meeting in the middle.

For a man who had always been the provider, the protector, the leader, so much had been taken. But to my son, he wasn't just a failing memory. He was still a father. Still a grandfather. Still giving.

Sometimes, I forgot that. In the daily, demanding need of caregiving, I watched my father's every move. I made sure he dressed for the weather. I anticipated his needs before he even realized them himself. I clung to the structure I had built because, if I let go even for a moment, I feared I'd drown. And the truth is, sometimes I did.

But I stayed present in the heat of that day, my son's laughter and my dad's washing over me. I let the moment be.

Even if the names went soft, I knew this bridge would hold.

Chapter 14

Routines & Reinforcements

I heard him before I saw him, the careful shuffle in the hall, then the soft close of a door. The throat clear—his way of letting me know he was ready to be found. I followed those sounds down the hallway. When I stepped into his room, he was sitting at the edge of the bed in his undershirt, socks half on, studying the shoelaces of his blue and white New Balances like an old map.

"Morning, Dad."

"Hey, Tahn," he said, bright already. "What's for breakfast?"

"Coffee first. Then Raisin Bran. Maybe eggs if I'm feelin up to it."

"You will," he said, confident.

We kept to the routine we had come to trust. Lotion across the backs of his hands. Deodorant. A clean T-shirt. I set his jeans in his lap, and he nodded like I'd handed him a small assignment he was pleased to accept. I knelt beside him, helped him wiggle his shoe on, then waited. There were days he could tie them on his own, and other days he needed help. Today, he did it on his own.

"Got it," he said, grinning from the accomplishment.

"Great, let's go get some grub!"

Every morning at breakfast, I found myself waiting to see which memory would push through that day. His mind, though fractured, held on to the pieces that mattered to him the most.

He sniffed as he entered the kitchen, eyes brightening. "That ham?"

"Just a little." I cracked two eggs and let the edges lace.

He leaned in, casually. "Couldn't eat pork in our house. My mother didn't let us." A smile tugged his mouth. "So, ya see what we did was . . . slide next door. The lady next to our house made me a ham sandwich on that soft bread. Mayo. Little mustard. Cut on the diagonal. It was our secret." He chuckled. "We never told my mother."

"Wow," I said, setting down his plate. "Rebel."

"No, no, we were hungry," he corrected.

"Got it. Well, after you eat," I said lightly, "we have a visitor coming today. Her name is Carla. She's coming to help me keep things together."

"Carla," he repeated, testing it. "Alright then."

He ate the eggs slow and happy, then folded a slice of toast with jelly like it was a second course at a diner he loved. Between sips of coffee, he sang along to a Ray Charles song under his breath. "*I got a woman, way over town that's good to me. . .*"

The words came out in order, right where they belonged, his foot tapping under the table, fingers drumming once against the mug. No searching. No stopping. No starting over. Those were good mornings.

I finished the dishes, and we moved to the small work of being alive. A short walk to the slider to look out at the yard. The maple tossed coin-shaped light over the grass. He took in the scene like a foreman checking his site. Then off to the family room for his favorite show. *Gunsmoke.*

The morning became afternoon, and Carla arrived with a tote and warm eyes that knew the terrain. I escorted her in and invited her to the kitchen table. As I poured coffee, she opened a leather folder and took in the room.

"Tell me about your best days," she said.

"Well," I answered. "He eats. He jokes. We walk the neighborhood. TV. Nap. Dinner. Early to bed."

"And the hard parts?"

"Med refusals. Sun-downing. Wandering if I blink too long. Nights where there's no sleep to be had."

Carla nodded. "If there are areas of concern with your routine, I am here to help you with that and especially how to navigate outside assistance."

"As you can see," I began, activating business mode, "I've already labeled the doors. This house has too many. I even get lost in it sometimes. I added locks at the top of the exits, so we don't have another find-your-father moment. Pills are organized. This binder has all his information and space for notes." I stopped, knowing I'd reached out to Carla for more than a rundown of the systems I already had in place. "What I need is help," I admitted. "My days are constantly interrupted by his mind. He can sit for an hour with his westerns, and I squeeze in a meeting, but then I am back on. I'm walking on eggshells, always on alert."

Dad wandered in from the family room and studied Carla as her pen moved. "What's going on here?"

She smiled. "Just helping your daughter with some planning." Then she whispered in my direction. "You are doing an excellent job. Let's give your nervous system a place to sit."

"I'm not here to fix your routine," she said, flipping open a pad. "You've got one. I'm here to get you paid help without bleeding your own wallet. That means Medicaid home care."

"Good," I said. "Because out of pocket is breaking me."

She nodded. "Okay. Here's the road map."

She drew three boxes on her pad and wrote in bold:

1. Eligibility
2. Assessment
3. Services Start

"Box one is financial and legal," she said. "You already have POA and HIPAA in a grab-folder—gold. Now, we prove he qualifies financially for Community Medicaid home care in our state."

"What does that actually mean?" I asked.

"Two pieces," she said, counting on her fingers. "Assets and income. Assets: We list everything with his name on it—checking, savings, CDs, life policies with cash value, retirement accounts, the house, car. Some things are generally non-countable or treated differently. Primary residence up to program rules, one car, personal items, and pre-paid burial. Everything else we either need to spend down legitimately on his needs or plan around with the elder-law attorney."

"And income?"

"If monthly income is above the Medicaid limit, you don't get denied, you create a 'spend-down' or use a pooled income trust, so his surplus pays approved bills and he keeps eligibility. I'll connect you with a trust administrator; the attorney can set it up fast."

She turned the page.

"Documents you'll pull this week," she said, sliding me a checklist. "IDs, SS card, Medicare card, supplemental insurance card, POA, birth certificate if you have it, marriage certificate if relevant, recent bank statements, proof of any pensions or Social Security, deed or property tax bill, car registration, life policy statement, retirement statements, and a list of current meds and doctors. If something's missing, we file and supplement; don't let paperwork perfection slow you down."

"Where does the application go?" I asked.

"Local DSS/Medicaid office," she said. "We submit the Community Medicaid application, plus a physician's order that confirms he needs help at home. While the financial side is being reviewed, we move on to box two, functional assessment, so we don't lose time."

She drew arrows to box two, continuing her explanation.

"Assessment has two parts: First, his doctor signs the home-care order and summary. Second, a nurse comes to the house for a

UAS assessment. They'll watch transfers, bathing, dressing, eating, meds, cognition, and safety. That score helps set hours."

"He's cooperative most mornings," I said. "Afternoons can tilt."

"Then we book the assessment for the morning," she said. "I'll coach you on language and be truthful about bad days. No hero stories. If you step in for him, tell the nurse that's not his independent baseline."

She wrote MLTC in the margin.

I watched the pen move, trying to hold onto each step as she said it, knowing I wouldn't remember half of it later.

"After approval, you choose a Managed Long-Term Care plan. They'll do one more visit and authorize hours. Two service models: traditional home-care agency or CDPAP."

"Explain CDPAP like I'm sleep-deprived," I said, the acronyms already crowding my head, one pushing out the next.

"CDPAP lets a family member or friend be the paid aide—not a spouse. The plan pays a fiscal intermediary; they handle payroll. If you pick agency care, the plan sends their aides. Either way, there's electronic visit verification. We start with a safe number of hours and appeal for more if needed."

I nodded, trying to track it.

Agency.

CDPAP.

Hours.

Appeal.

He shuffled in then, coffee mug in hand, catching only the last line. "Appeal what?"

"More help," I said. "So, we can get you someone else to look at other than me." And gave him a wink.

He smiled at that, satisfied, and drifted back to *Gunsmoke*.

Carla lowered her voice. "While this moves, keep paying for only what keeps him safe—no guilt buys. Medicaid won't reimburse retroactively for private aides unless you're in a very specific program, so we have to run lean for a few weeks."

A few weeks!

"How long til help shows up?" I asked. I needed it now; the process Carla was describing sounded far longer than that.

"Depends on the county and how fast we feed the beast," she said, which didn't reassure me. "You're organized, so we can push. Here's the order to expect: application filed, doctor order in, nurse assessment done, financial pending, MLTC chosen, hours authorized, start of care. I'll quarterback the sequence and chase people when they stall."

The list stacked up, one step on top of the next, already slipping.

"What about the house?" I asked. "We're planning to sell my parents' home next."

"That's attorney territory," she said. "He'll make sure the sale and proceeds are handled within Medicaid rules—think exempt spend-downs, repairs, pre-paid burial, possible trust work—so that eligibility stays intact. Your job is to keep clean records. Keep receipts. Keep logs. Annual redetermination comes fast."

Keep. Keep. Keep.

She slid the checklist toward me, then wrote one last line at the bottom before handing it over: Keep a crisis folder by the door.

"What's in that?"

"Photocopies of ID, POA, meds list, diagnoses, allergy list, recent vitals, names and numbers for me, the MLTC, and his doctors. If EMS shows up, you hand them that folder. If a new aide walks in, you hand them the folder. It keeps you from telling the same story five times a day."

I pictured it already—paper stacked, clipped, waiting by the door like something we'd need sooner than we wanted.

I exhaled. "This is the first conversation that feels like traction."

"It is traction," she said, standing. "You've already done the hardest part. Now we plug you into a system that should have found you first."

After she left, I stacked the papers into three neat piles and labeled them: File Now, Call Today, and Ask Attorney.

The dogs settled at my feet. Dad sat in his chair, *Gunsmoke* playing low, daylight from the window falling across his face. His mug rested in his hand, forgotten between sips.

The house felt held. Not by hope, no, but by process. I would become a logistics master. I would get the help I needed.

Two days later, I sat alone in the elder-law conference room with my "Fast Eddie Binder," a comprehensive guide to his care. It held everything: medications, doctors' visits with notes, finances, sleeping patterns, bathroom schedules. Every detail, every contingency, documented and controlled. We reviewed the plan like a playbook: confirm Community Medicaid path, prepare pooled income trust packet, draft a simple caregiver agreement so payments for my time and mileage are clean, map how the house sale proceeds will be handled so eligibility doesn't blow up. I signed the engagement letter, slid my copies into the folder, and walked out with dates on the calendar.

When I got home, *Gilligan's Island* was on in the family room. Dad sat tucked under a blanket, pudding cup in hand, eyes soft and warm. I slid in beside him and kept it plain. "Hey, Dad. I lined up people to help me take care of things. The house. Some help here. It's set."

He glanced at the TV, then back to me. A small nod. "Alright then."

"How's that sound?"

"Good to me." His words landed certain, like a supportive hand between my shoulders. "You'll handle it."

"I will." I was confident.

He scooped a little pudding and held the spoon out to me like I was still his little kid. "You want some?"

"Thanks, I'm good. Watching my figure," I said, grinning.

He chuckled, pleased with both of us. I felt my body let go of the tension it had been holding. We watched the Skipper yell at Gilligan while the spoon scraped the last bit of chocolate from the cup. And with his shoulder against mine, the laugh track rolling, I felt it; the small, certain feeling that for this minute we had what we needed. That was enough.

Chapter 15

Unsaid

By late 2021, almost two years in, the days had a structure again. Paperwork moved when it was supposed to. Calls were returned. Medicaid was finally in place, and we were pushing through the next layer, getting Brianna set up as a paid caregiver through CDPAP, which came with its own set of fights.

The systems were running. Not smoothly, but predictably.

I let myself believe we had found our footing.

Occasionally, my mother and sister would come up together on random weekends so Darius and I could get away. Nothing extravagant. We'd stay at a local hotel, catch a comedy show, then have dinner somewhere close enough that we wouldn't talk ourselves out of going.

We attempted to retrieve something that had slowly begun to fray. A few carefully arranged hours where the house didn't need us. Where our marriage might remember itself.

"Are we doing a fancy dinner?" Darius yelled from the upstairs room.

"No," I said, packing clothes into my red suitcase. "Just going to The Standard. It's close to the hotel. Then we'll head to the show."

I carried my bag downstairs and placed it next to the garage door as the doorbell rang.

My sister stood there, overnight bag in hand, my mother hovering just behind her, coat still zipped, already trying to maneuver around the dogs who were blocking the doorway with more enthusiasm than coordination.

Dad was on his feet before I could move. His face lit up like something important was about to happen.

The dogs circled, nails clicking, bodies wiggling, thrilled by the disruption. Dad laughed, reaching down to pet whichever one landed closest.

He wrapped my sister in a hug, grinning wide. "Come on in. Good to see ya."

Like he hadn't seen her in years instead of just three weeks earlier.

But every visit was new to him now.

"Good to see you, Dad," my sister said. "You look good."

"Here, Tahnya," my mother said, already handing me her bag. "Take this upstairs for me."

Darius came down with his suitcase just in time for us to switch. He grabbed my mother's bag. I grabbed his. I set his bag next to mine, the car waiting for our getaway.

We looked like a couple trying to escape a prison. Moving fast.

"I made chicken and a salad for Dad," I said quickly, slipping into instruction mode while I put on my coat. "He probably won't eat the salad. He's got a thing against anything green now. His meds are crushed. Pill crusher is on the counter. You can mix them into the vanilla ice cream or the pudding in the fridge. Just watch him."

My sister raised an eyebrow. "Watch him how?"

"He'll hide the spoon and the cup in his pocket," I said. "You might have to coax them out of him. If not, I'll find them in three days when a line of ants leads me straight to it."

She laughed. "Okay. We've got this. Go. Have fun."

Out the door we went, like parents leaving their kids with a sitter. Excited and exhausted at the same time.

Our ride to the hotel was without words. It needed to be. This was our chance to rest. To reset. As we pulled up, Darius dropped me at the front door.

"I'll get us checked in; you got the bags?" I asked, more like an instruction than a question.

"Yup, I got em."

I watched him pull away and head toward the far end of the lot. Far enough to feel punitive.

He walked into the hotel a few minutes later with that look. The one everyone loved. Perfect jeans. Casual boots. A dark blue sweater over a pressed collared shirt.

Handsome, I thought.

But that smile—the one that had drawn me in years ago, approachable and friendly—had started to irritate me.

In that moment, though, watching him walk toward me, I remembered.

Dating him.

Our backyard wedding.

The house we shared.

Us, before everything hardened.

Hope brushed past me. Light. Brief. Dangerous.

He held the elevator door open for me, rolled our bags behind him as we found our room. We hung up our coats and slid the suitcases into the closet.

We'd made it; a weekend away with no interruptions.

The room was chilly, typical for the time of year. But the bed was made. And no one needed anything from us. I went into the bathroom to check my hair, put on my makeup, and then off we went.

I was ready to order when our waitress approached. She said her name, but I didn't hear it, nor did I care. "Pinot Grigio, please."

"And for you sir?" the waitress asked Darius, hoping he would be easier than me.

"Do you have iced tea?" he responded, smiling.

"Unsweetened," she said, like an apology.

"That's fine," he said. "I'll add sugar."

"You look nice," he said after the waitress walked away.

I looked up. "Thank you."

"You do." trying to convince me.

I smiled into my wine glass, unsure what to do with the compliment.

We used to talk for hours. That night, we struggled to fill ten minutes.

At the show, we were escorted to our seats, dead center in front of the stage. The comedian entered, and the crowd welcomed him with a roar of applause. Although the club was small, it felt like an arena. We settled in, laughter peppering the room as he began his set.

"I can resolve any marital issues," the comic declared at one point in the show.

I chuckled. *Yeah, okay.*

"Who here has an issue?"

Something inside me decided to volunteer.

"He always snores," I blurted out.

The comic stared at Darius for a moment, then smiled. "Did he snore when you met him?"

"No," I responded quickly.

"That's because you sucked the life out of him!"

The crowd exploded. I laughed too. Harder than I meant to. Somewhere inside, I knew he wasn't wrong.

The rest of the show was exactly what I needed. I was laughing and light, something I hadn't felt in a long time.

No monitors.

No medications lined up in my head.

No listening for movement in another room.

Just noise. Laughter. People pressed close together.

I didn't have to watch anything. I didn't have to anticipate disaster.

And when the realization hit, it didn't feel like relief.

It felt like grief.

For the life we had before all of this.

The ease of it.

The way a night like this didn't have an edge to it.

I wondered if he'd felt it too.

The house.

What we thought we were building.

The start we thought we were getting.

Walking back to the hotel, the air cold enough to wake us up, Darius reached for my hand, and I allowed it.

It wasn't a small thing.

We walked in silence, our steps uneven on the sidewalk. His hand warm. Mine was freezing.

He hadn't always met me where I was. Not in the moments

that mattered most. Not when the weight of it all pressed in, and I needed him to take some of it without being asked.

He stayed just outside of it sometimes. Close, but not inside the work of it. Not inside the decisions, the watching, the constant calculation.

But he never left.

He carried what he knew how to carry. Made space where he could. Kept things moving when I was buried in it.

And I could feel it then, in the way his hand found mine. Not asking for anything. Not fixing anything. Just there.

I took his hand and held it.

It wasn't forgiveness, it wasn't resolution. It was me allowing space to hold it all.

What he was to me.

What he may never be.

Back in the hotel room, we got ready for bed in silence. The familiar choreography of brushing teeth, setting alarms, and climbing under separate sides of the blanket.

No phones. No talking. Just sleep that came fast and heavy.

Driving home the next day, Darius drove, one hand on the wheel, that smile still there, like something had stayed with him.

I caught it in the corner of my eye.

Like he'd had a reset.

I hadn't.

I knew what I was going back to.

By the time we pulled into the garage, I could feel it waiting for me.

The house greeted us before anyone spoke.

The dogs skidded across the floor when we opened the door, nails scraping, bodies colliding. Dad was already standing in the living room, coat half on, like he'd been waiting for us the whole time.

"There you are," he said, smiling wide. "Where'd you two go?"

I dropped my bag by the door. "Just away for the night, Dad. We went to see a comedy show."

"Oh," he said, nodding. "That's good. You should do that."

My mother was in the kitchen, rinsing a coffee mug. She didn't turn around right away.

"You guys have a nice time?" she asked, still focused on the sink.

"Yeah," I said. "It was good."

She set the mug in the dishwasher as I stepped into the kitchen, already scanning. Meds. Counters. Nothing out of place. My body transitioning into go-mode automatically.

Dad wandered toward the dogs, distracted. Darius squeezed my shoulder once, smiled, and carried the bags upstairs.

That's when she started dropping the hints.

"I've been thinkin'," she said, finally turning to face me.

I leaned against the counter, arms crossed, waiting.

"I think you need help." She said it like she was talking to herself more than to me.

I nodded. Noncommittal.

"And your father," she added, lowering her voice. "He wants me closer."

I didn't answer right away. I opened the fridge. Took stock. Closed it again.

"But I don't want to leave," she said quickly, as if she'd gone too far. "All my friends are there. Haley's right across the bridge."

She watched my face when she said it. I kept it neutral.

Dad wandered back in. "Who's leaving?" he asked.

"No one," my mother said immediately. Too fast. "We're just talking."

"Oh," he said, satisfied. He patted the counter and drifted back toward the living room.

She exhaled. "Driving back and forth," she said, "I did it with my parents. It's a long drive. If you think it makes sense."

There it was.

She needed me to say it. To give the approval. To make it something she could repeat later with certainty. That it was my idea. That I asked.

I made myself some coffee. Sat down at the table, slightly annoyed that she couldn't just say it. She saw what I was carrying. The relentless caretaking, the exhaustion, the small sacrifices that added up to a life almost entirely consumed by his needs. And I think, in some way, she wanted to reclaim a role in his story.

But the move? That was her decision. This was her husband. I wouldn't stand in her way if she wanted to be closer to him.

"We can look at places," I said.

She nodded, relieved and restrained at the same time. "I'm not saying I'm ready."

"I know."

She smiled, just enough.

So, while she talked in circles, planting seeds that had already taken root, I went to work behind the scenes. I researched communities late that night, laptop balanced on my knees while everyone else was sleeping. I already knew what she'd want without her saying a thing. To her, too, I was the fixer. The one who took action before anyone else did.

My mother and I had never been good. Not as a child. Not now.

With her, nothing ever came straight.

It came sideways.

In pieces.

In suggestions that weren't really suggestions.

She could say something sharp and then move on like she hadn't. Like I hadn't just felt it land.

And I didn't always let it go.

There were fights. Loud ones.

Me yelling back.

Telling her to stop. To get out. To leave me alone.

It never changed anything.

But not here.

Not with him in the next room.

His mind already slipping.

Already confused enough.

The last thing he needed was the two of us detonating in front of him.

So I held it.

Even when she pushed.

Even when I felt it building.

Like a powder keg I was standing on top of, pretending it wasn't there.

People saw it.

Friends who had known me forever. Others who barely knew her. It didn't matter. They all said some version of the same thing.

I don't know how you do it.

I wish she understood how much you do.

Standing there, listening to her circle it again, I could feel it happen without thinking.

I shut her out.

Kept it in.

The place needed to be close but familiar. Somewhere that

didn't feel like an ending. Somewhere, she could convince herself she was downsizing, not disappearing.

My search continued alongside my daily caregiving routines. On weekends, Dad and I would venture out for tours. We moved slowly through models, commenting on paint colors, closet doors, and how loud the floors or hallways sounded.

"Dad, what did you think of that one?"

"She would like this one," he said without hesitation.

"I think this is the one," I confirmed. "It's two minutes from the house. We could walk here if we wanted to."

"Is that right?" he answered with a small grin on his face.

"Yeah, but we won't be doing that!"

We both chuckled.

Two minutes felt like a compromise my mom and I could live with. It was close enough to check on her. Close enough for her to feel useful. And close enough for her to tell herself she was doing this for me.

So, we leapt. We had Mom come up one weekend and see the place, and she liked it. The paperwork moved faster than her emotions. Boxes checked. Forms signed. Within weeks, she had moved into her new two-bedroom apartment with big windows, a laundry room, and just enough space to hold onto the version of herself she still believed she was.

The next step to fit into my daily routines and late-night to-dos: selling their house.

Chapter 16

Roundtree Court

As we walked into the vestibule of my mother's new place, red decorations lined the hallways. Each resident had staked a small claim outside their door with a wreath, a sign, something to mark the season. My father walked a few steps behind me, holding a bouquet of flowers.

"Dad," I said, slowing down. "Go ahead. Knock."

He hesitated. Not sure who would answer. Not sure why he had the flowers. Then he knocked.

My mother opened the door and stopped short when she saw them.

"Oh," she said. "It's you."

My father handed them to her, still a little bewildered himself. "These are for you."

"Happy Valentine's Day," I whispered in his ear.

"Oh, yeah, Happy Valentine's Day." And he gently leaned in and kissed her cheek. For a moment, he remembered.

Inside, the apartment was taking shape. Furniture placed but not settled. Boxes half-opened. The outline of a life not quite filled in yet. There was still so much to do.

My mother poured wine into a plastic cup and handed it to me. I found a real glass, rinsed it out, and took a sip.

"I'm going to have to make a lot of trips back and forth to get the house ready to sell," I said. "You can come with me some weekends if you want. But I think it might be best if you stay here and help Darius with Dad while I'm gone."

"I know," she said. "Did you talk to Patty? It would be great if she could help us sell the house."

"I left her a message," I said, already steps ahead. "I'm going to get her a key so she can take a look and get it listed. I'm heading down again next weekend, if the weather cooperates."

"Tahn," my father said suddenly, his voice bright, almost clear. "What are you talking about?"

"We're selling the house in Beacon, Dad," I said. "Mom lives here now, so she can come see you more often."

He turned to her. "Is that right? You live here, Peach?"

"Yes," she said quickly. "You know that. You were here when I moved in. You helped Tahnya find it."

She said, 'You know' the way she always did. As if repeating the facts could make them true for him again. Sometimes it worked. More often, it sent him searching through a reel of memories that didn't match the room he was standing in.

"Mom," I said, stepping in, "we'll figure out weekends once I talk to Patty and get next steps. For now, I'll go down when I can and when I have help for Dad."

"Okay," she said.

I was surprised how easily she agreed.

From there, days became an exercise in pacing. Everything was a balance. My father's care. My mother's transition. Weekends carved into pieces so I could drive back and forth to pack up forty-plus years of belongings. I preferred doing most of it without her. My sister met me when she could. Other times, someone from my tribe showed up, sleeves rolled, ready to lift what needed lifting.

Back home, my house had become a sanctuary. A staycation space for my mother, for visitors, for the rotating door of people who would pass through over the next two years. I relied on that circle while I was gone. Lisette, one of my best friends, a part of my tribe, moved in while she searched for an apartment upstate. Collin was there with his girlfriend, Angel. Darius, too, of course.

Everyone knew the routines. Everyone understood the rules. The house ran on my father's needs. Everyone else learned the orbit.

So, I started splitting my life between two homes.

It was an hour and a half each way to my parents' old house. I had Comfort Inn on speed dial and the Fast Eddie Binder riding shotgun like a co-pilot with opinions. By the third trip, the front-desk woman called me *hon*. I learned which rooms had heaters that clattered and which ones hissed. At night, I spread the binder across the narrow desk, lined up the next day's calls—realtor, lawyer, benefits office—and let the ceiling talk me to sleep.

We didn't audition the house. No paint. No staging.

Patty, our realtor, was a friend who had lived in the same row of townhomes. I got her a key. She added the lock box that weekend.

I was driving home after a weekend of packing as much as I could lift and wedge into my car, singing Whitney Houston at the top of my lungs, when my phone rang.

"Hey, Tahnya. How's it going? How are your mom and dad?"

"Pretty good. I'm driving back. Did you get a chance to go in?"

"Yeah," she said. "I'm standing in the driveway. List it as is," she continued. "Don't fix a thing. Investors are buying these. Goal is simple. Empty it. I'll push it Thursday. Expect offers by Monday."

When I got home, I wrote **EMPTY IT** at the top of my pad and underlined it twice.

It felt like permission and a dare.

A neighbor down the block, a legal secretary, efficient as a stapler, routed me to a real estate law office that spoke in bullet points and deadlines. Most of it happened by phone. I scanned. I signed. I hole-punched. Community Medicaid was already in motion. Excess income would flow through the pooled trust. Eligibility would stay intact. Bills would get paid.

One rule ran through my head on repeat:

Move clean. Move fast. Don't get cute.

The work on the ground was boxes, exhaustion, and weight.

Sometimes my mother came with me. She stayed with my sister, and I'd pick her up before heading to the house to finish packing. By the time I unlocked the door, I was already bracing for impact. The battle of what to keep and what to get rid of started almost immediately. We didn't argue in speeches. We argued in objects.

The casserole dish had a personality.

That lamp had stood starboard since 1989.

The metal rack that held wood for the stove, empty now, still insisting it mattered.

Three piles became five: keep, donate, toss, decide later, decide later again.

"You're moving too fast," she said, hands on her hips.

"We have four weekends," I said, ripping packing tape with my teeth.

"Why are you always so nasty? You make everything sound urgent."

"It is," I said. "This has to get done. Fast."

I didn't say the rest.

I didn't remind her that other people were caring for my father while I spent my weekends hauling her life into boxes. That her new apartment was half the size of their old place, and nothing would fit. That I was doing math every minute. Time. Money. Space. Patience.

She tried to regain control by contradicting small facts.

I let the small facts go.

I wrapped picture frames in newspaper she had already read. I stacked photo albums spine-up so she could spot them and know what I'd packed where without asking.

Quiet would settle for ten minutes, then she would unearth a relic and retell a right memory with the wrong date. I let it pass.

The truer thing was this: she was handing me her life in fist-sized pieces and trying not to look at the Toss pile.

The house was already half echo. Cabinet doors sounded too loud. Lemon Pledge hung in the air because I'd overdone it. My mother stood in the doorway with a grocery bag like we might still need to feed the place.

"Just a few last things," she said, which had never once been true.

We moved from room to room without ceremony. I opened the junk drawer. Raffle stubs. Brittle rubber bands. A key we never identified. She reached for it. I let her take it.

In the living room, she pulled a paperback from the shelf. "Your father liked this one."

Between rooms, I tried to keep working. I took calls in the empty hallway and wrote with a pencil because pens track when you're tired. My phone vibrated constantly.

Patty's name appeared again.

Her voice carried momentum. Inventory thin. Rents up. Cash buyers circling.

"This is priced perfectly," she said. "I already have offers. You might get a bidding war. How long until everything's out? Fast is our friend."

The bids came in like weather fronts. Clean offers. Short inspections. Quick closes.

Patty texted screenshots, then called.

"Pick the one whose money arrives like a Swiss train."

We did.

I didn't show my mother the stack of offers. I showed her the outcome of my efforts.

"This keeps you housed," I said, my finger on the number. "This pays for help."

She nodded. A small nod that meant *yes,* and *don't make me say more.*

And like that, it was done. We had a buyer and a closing date set for spring.

The day before closing, the block showed up for a send-off. Snacks and paper plates. Coolers filled with soda, water, wine, and beer. The house smelled like a tinge of dusty old carpet and the bleach cleaner we always overused before company.

I took one slow lap through the house before my father arrived with Darius. I stood in the bathroom where I practiced speeches for a life I never lived. The living room where my father once fell asleep fully dressed after a double shift. I rested my hand on the wood-burning stove like I was checking a pulse. I studied the spot on the wall where an array of school photos used to hang, always a little crooked. All of it still there in my mind, in the memories of that house, and all of it gone.

When I emerged from the house, the driveway had turned into memory lane, overflowing with hugs, lawn chairs, and fond farewells. Stories told three ways. The feel of community losing a pair of its original founders. Darius arrived with my father, and the yard erupted into smiles and greetings as everyone rearranged themselves to be around him. He hadn't been there since he came to live with us, and his return felt like a celebrity coming home after their big break.

He laughed like each memory was brand new. Commented on shoes, hair, and who still looked the same. I am not sure what he actually remembered or if he was just acting; somewhere in his mind, he knew this "party" was for him, but I don't think he was quite sure why.

God help me if he thinks he's finally back home and wants to stay, I thought, watching the joy on his face. *How the hell are we gonna get him back in the car?*

But that didn't happen. The day was wonderful, and we could feel the love from the neighborhood that raised us.

"Hey, Dad, you wanna go inside and take one last look around?" I asked. Darius was taking him back so that I could be at the closing the next day, but I wanted to give him a chance to say goodbye.

"Sure, let's go."

We entered the now empty house with just a few boxes remaining in the corner.

"Where did everything go?" he said, his voice curious.

"We moved it all into mom's new apartment, and the rest of it is in your new bedroom at my house. We're going to live there from now on. Lots of new memories and celebrations. That party out there is for you and mom to celebrate your new chapter."

"Oh, is that right?" He said with a grin and a wandering eye as he gazed around what was once the living room.

I walked him through to the backyard, and my mother joined us. The three of us took in the space where she had grown her gardens full of tomatoes and where he had split and stacked wood for the fire. They stopped to take a picture. We went back inside, then upstairs to the bedroom that had once been mine. The chimney cut through the middle back of the room, the way it always had. His books lined the shelves. His things filled the space. Mine buried underneath, frozen in time.

He pointed. "Those are all my books."

"Yup," I confirmed, "and I'm gonna have Darius bring them home with you today and put them in your room."

"Oh, that sounds good."

Relief moved through me so fast I almost missed it. He wasn't going to put up a fight and want to stay; he would go back with Darius without issue. I knew I had to take these small wins in the tumbling onslaught of staying one step ahead of his mind. But my body was so sleep-deprived these days, my brain so focused, that it barely registered.

Outside, my mother floated, laughing with neighbors, repeating how much she didn't want to move, how I needed her help. Each time I heard it, I flinched.

Dusk settled in, and old neighbors retreated to their homes. My sister and I went back inside one more time.

This was it. We were saying goodbye to our past.

She walked over to the wood-burning stove and said, "Take a picture, this is one we have to always remember."

"How could we ever forget?" I exclaimed.

We met Mom, Dad, and Darius at the end of the driveway and took one more picture of us as a family. I waved them off, then went back in to lock up. I placed the keys on the kitchen counter.

House. Shed. The extra ones we never solved.

I moved through the rooms one last time, alone, turning off lights as I went. The living room. The upstairs hallway. The kitchen. Each click felt louder than it should have.

At the front door, I paused. Not to look back. Just to let the shape of the place pass through me.

One last click for the outside light. Then I stepped outside and closed the door.

Chapter 17

A Familiar Ease

We had missed celebrating my parents' birthdays, born a day apart and both now seventy-eight, because of the closing. But we decided to do something small anyway.

Which, in our family, meant hosting about sixty people.

My mother thought she was coming over to help me plant tomatoes. I had agreed to a garden when she moved up, partly because she wanted it, and partly because I wanted my father to have something familiar to do once the weather finally broke. Something with dirt and purpose.

What she didn't know was that the backyard was already full.

I had been herding people around for twenty minutes. Whispering. Waving my arms. Pointing. Shuffling bodies onto the deck like a stage manager trying to save opening night.

"No, not there, behind the grill. Shoes off if you're on the steps. Quiet. Quiet. QUIET."

People crouched. People hid behind planters. Someone laughed too loud and I shot them a look that shut it down immediately. My heart was pounding so hard I could feel the pressure behind my eyes.

Brianna met my mother in the driveway right on cue.

She took her arm casually, like nothing unusual was happening, and walked her around back.

I stood on the deck, hands raised, counting down in my head.

Three.

Two.

They cleared the corner.

"SURPRISE!"

The sound hit like a wave. Sixty voices, full volume. My mother jumped so hard I thought she might levitate. Her hand flew to her chest. Her mouth opened. Closed. Opened again.

"Oh my God," she said. "Oh my God."

Everyone laughed. Someone clapped. Someone else yelled "Happy Birthday!" from the back like they couldn't contain it.

My father stood just off to the side, watching. Not startled. Not confused. Just taking it in. He smiled, slow and wide, like he knew this moment mattered even if he couldn't quite place why.

The backyard was full of family, friends, and new neighbors she was still learning the names of. There were folding tables and coolers. Chairs pulled too close together. It felt intentional in the way crowded things sometimes do. Like a decision had been made.

This was home now.

Stories rolled out, the same ones that had filled the driveway at Roundtree Court a few weeks before, picking up where they left off. My father drifted from group to group, mostly quiet but comfortable, still the storyteller when prompted, still the entertainer when someone gave him an opening. His charm bright enough to make you forget.

Me? I kept moving.

Refilling drinks. Answering questions. Making sure everyone had what they needed. Hosting on autopilot. When I finally felt the crowd settle into itself, I found my father and stayed close.

That's when Bri stepped in beside him. Without hesitation. Unannounced. Like she'd always been there.

The sight of her beside him pulled me backward.

Years earlier. Summer thick in the air. Bri running toward me with one of the older kids on the block, screaming, blood on her chin, her tiny body vibrating with pain and panic. She was five. My heart dropped. The neighborhood tilted.

My father came down the driveway.

He didn't rush. He didn't flail. He just walked toward her, unaffected, like his body already knew what to do. He knelt beside her, knowing exactly what to do.

"It's okay, Bri," he said. "Let me see."

Two teeth were gone, and her lip was swelling.

My fear wanted to sprint. His voice made her stop long enough to breathe.

"We have to get her to the ER in case she broke something," he said. "I can't tell where the blood is coming from."

In the back seat, he held a paper towel to her mouth and whispered nonsense meant only to distract. At the ER, she was half-asleep when she pulled another tooth from her mouth, held it up to him, and said, "Here, Grandpa."

That made him laugh. Soft. Warm. Not rushed.

Bri smiled back, eased by then, like his laugh had rewired something inside her. She handed him the tooth, and he accepted it like a promise.

When he laughed like that, the world didn't feel broken. It felt predictable. Safe.

Years later, when she would steady him with a hand at his back, when she would coax him through fear with platitudes and patience, I would recognize that smile.

It had started there. With a tooth. With trust. With a laugh that told her she was safe.

And standing in my backyard now, watching Bri move easily at his side, I understood something I hadn't named before.

She had learned care then. Long before diagnoses. Long before binders and pill crushers and night cameras. She learned it the day she ran toward us, bleeding and afraid, and he soothed her instead of panicking. She learned it in the way he steadied her first, and in how she never forgot what that felt like.

This was not new for her.

It was remembered.

She didn't hover over him. She didn't announce herself. She adjusted his chair without asking. Handed him a drink before he realized he was thirsty. Laughed at the right moment. Redirected without correcting. Stayed close without crowding. It was instinctive, like muscle memory.

I watched them together and felt something land deep before I could name it.

The sense that something heavy had been set down—not abandoned but now shared.

Brianna became his paid caregiver through CDPAP in early 2022, taking scheduled shifts that slowly became the architecture of our days. By the time she was fully woven into the routine, it had already become part of her.

She became his caregiver not because she had to, but because she could. Because she knew how to meet him where he was with her quick wit instead of force, with tenderness instead of fear. She knew how to make him laugh, how to calm him, how to see him when the rest of the world only saw decline.

She called him Gramps. Not as a nickname but as a language they shared.

She made sure he listened to his music. Played his old records. Danced with him in the living room when his body still allowed it. Westerns became their ritual. At first, she watched because he loved them. Then she watched because she did. She learned every character, every line that made him laugh. He wasn't just her grandfather. He was her companion in a world they built together, piece by piece.

Because of her, I could start to breathe again.

I could step away without fear. I could sleep without listening for footsteps. I could leave the house knowing he was not just supervised but understood.

She gave him what no agency ever could. Family. Familiarity. Warmth.

And she gave me something too.

The first true sense that I was no longer doing this alone.

Chapter 18

The System

For as easy as it was for Bri to step into the caregiving role, getting her set up as a paid family caregiver through the system was, in a word, hell.

Medicaid did not make things easier; it did exactly the opposite. Every rule seemed designed to catch you doing the wrong thing, even when you were doing the only thing that made sense. The system isn't built for families like ours, families who want to be involved in their loved ones' care. It punishes you for stepping up.

I learned early on that I could not be both my father's Power of Attorney and a paid caregiver. Which is absolute-bullshit.

Because when you have a man with Alzheimer's who needs care around the clock, someone has to be his voice. Someone has to manage his money, his medical decisions, his safety, his dignity. Someone has to make sure the lights stay on, the meds get filled, and the doors stay locked at night. That person is the Power of Attorney. And that same person is usually the one doing the work. The bathing. The redirecting. The cleaning. The watching. The not-sleeping.

But the system says you have to choose. Either you advocate, or you get paid. You can't do both.

I was losing clients. Losing money by the boatloads. Losing my mind. If it weren't for Bri stepping in, I don't know how long my business would have lasted.

The process itself felt like a test of endurance.

Fax after fax. Yes, faxes. In 2022.

Forms that contradicted each other. Calls where I explained our situation from the beginning, again, to a new voice every time. "Can you tell me when the diagnosis began?" "Can you verify his level of impairment?" "Has there been a change since last month?" Every question assumed stability. None accounted for the decline.

One afternoon, after being on hold for forty-seven minutes, a woman on the other end of the line told me a document was missing.

"I sent that," I said, flipping through my binder. "Twice."

"Well, it's not here."

"Can you tell me what happens if it doesn't arrive?"

She paused. "We close the request."

I remember gripping the phone so hard my hand went numb. "So just to be clear," I said slowly, "if your machine eats my fax, my father doesn't get care."

Another pause. "You can always reapply."

Reapply. As if this were a library card.

When Bri was finally approved, my relief lasted for about twelve seconds before I spotted the hours.

Twenty.

Twenty hours of paid care per week.

I actually laughed. A sharp, humorless sound that startled my dog.

Twenty hours against the reality of one hundred and sixty-eight.

I called Carla immediately. She was kind. She was human. She told me the truth.

"We can appeal for more hours," she said. "But you'll need documentation from his physician."

I closed my eyes. "He wanders. He sundowns. He doesn't sleep. He thinks he's going home to West Virginia."

"Yes," she said gently. "But it has to be documented."

As if Alzheimer's needed footnotes.

So, I did the math.

I structured my life around those twenty hours like a chessboard. Bri came at eight in the morning. She got him up, dressed, through breakfast, through lunch. She prepped dinner so I could take over after work into the evening shift.

Every week, I had to choose.

Work or sleep.

Most weeks, I chose work.

Because losing sleep felt survivable. Losing my business and income did not.

But the nights were their own war.

He would fall asleep watching the news with Darius and me, have his spiked ice cream, then head to bed around nine. By ten-thirty, he'd be up again. Wandering. Opening doors. Convinced it was morning. Sometimes he wouldn't settle until after midnight. Sometimes one.

There is no off switch when you are responsible for someone else's safety. Your body never powers down. Your brain stays lit like a control room.

I had already spent years fighting for my father. Now I was fighting the systems that claimed they existed to help him.

So, I found the strength somewhere deep within to continue the fight. Because if I didn't, no one else would. And that was not an option.

Having Bri there during the day, and Darius, Collin, and Lisette living in the house, gave me just enough margin to function.

It was the closest I had come to what care should feel like—shared.

It reminded me of something I had noticed in 2021 while traveling through northern Spain, in Bilbao. Collin had gotten an offer to play soccer there, and I went with him, just the two of us.

While touring the city, I noticed older people weren't tucked away or rushed past. They moved slowly through the streets, arm in arm with someone younger—maybe a relative, maybe a companion, maybe just another human keeping pace. No one seemed embarrassed by it. No one acted like care was a disruption. It felt integrated. Normal. Public.

I don't know how they made it work. I only know what I saw.

This is how we should be living.

Not because aging is easier there, but because it isn't hidden. Care didn't seem like a private failure or an individual burden. It seemed understood. Expected. As if everyone knew this was part of the deal of being human: you age, and someone walks with you.

In the U.S., care feels like a problem we're supposed to solve quietly. Each of us is supposed to figure it out. Pay for it. Manage it. Not let it interfere with our lives or, especially, inconvenience anyone else's. But what I saw there suggested something different. That care isn't a question of *if* or *how*; it's an acceptance that we all arrive there eventually, and how we age depends entirely on who is allowed to help us along the way.

That contrast between countries, between cultures, stayed with me long after our trip to Spain.

Because what I observed in Bilbao wasn't about ease. It was about design. About care being woven into daily life instead of being fought for in private. About support that didn't require paperwork, proof, or permission.

Care isn't meant to be carried alone.

It takes a village. Not as a slogan. As a structure.

What my family and I were doing at home to care for my father was our own version of that. Improvised. Fragile. Held together by love and exhaustion—not systems or design.

Having that many people under one roof gave me just enough margin to keep going. It felt, briefly, like what I had seen in Spain. Not a miracle. Not a solution. Just shared weight.

For the first time in a long time, I could think about the future. Not in years. Not in plans. Just enough to imagine something beyond survival.

So, I planned a trip to Mexico for my fiftieth birthday.

One full week.

Seven days of sun, friends, food, and laughter.

No caregiving.

No vigilance.

No math.

For a moment, I imagined getting my life back. At least for seven days.

But even during the planning, I clearly understood something.

The system was not going to save us.

No policy was coming.

No relief was waiting on the other side of a form.

If this was going to work, it would be because *we* made it work.

No one was coming.

This was on me.

Chapter 19

Permission To Breathe

Planning was everything.

Not dreaming. Planning.

Every caregiver knows the difference.

I had been talking about my fiftieth birthday with Ninette for nearly two years. Half-joking at first. "We should do something big." But the closer it got, the more serious I became. I didn't want to mark this number from the kitchen table with one ear tuned for movement upstairs.

I wanted something fantastic.

And that meant having a plan. Not a wish. Not a hope. A plan built with precision that left no gaps unaccounted for.

Shifts covered.

Night coverage mapped.

Darius would be required to check in with honesty, not optimism. I even scheduled my sister to come for a few days so Darius wouldn't get overwhelmed.

The rest of the house assigned roles without debate.

Bri was my lifeline. Always steady. Always second in command. She was the reason I could even consider leaving. She understood my father. She understood me. She understood why every routine existed and why nothing could be skipped. She didn't see structure as a form of control. She saw it as care.

I knew nothing would fall apart while I was gone.

That mattered more than the plane ticket. More than seven days of freedom.

When you just have yourself to rely on—when it's just you ensuring someone else's world keeps turning—your own health stops existing. You become a conduit to someone else's care, your body a means to make ends meet. And it works for a while, because health doesn't disappear all at once. It slides. Slowly. You tell yourself it's temporary. You tell yourself you'll deal with it later.

But later doesn't come on its own.

I didn't realize how much my health had slipped until I was nearly fifty and my body started speaking up in ways I couldn't ignore. The athlete I had been in my teens and thirties was still there. Strong. Determined. Competitive with herself. She hadn't left. She'd been buried.

Two and a half years of caregiving, running a business, and managing the daily demands of everything in between had settled into my joints, my sleep, and my breath. I had gained weight, yes, but what scared me wasn't the mirror. It was the inflammation. The exhaustion. My body carried the consequences even when my eyes were closed.

Cortisol lived in my body. Fight or flight on repeat. Always listening. Always bracing. Always ready.

I made myself a promise. Nonnegotiable.

I would not let my body be the next thing to collapse.

So, I walked.

At first, it was practical. A park near my house. Sneakers. Headphones. Ten thousand steps as my goal because it sounded official enough to matter. I walked past the same trees, the same benches, the same couples pushing strollers. On hard days, when I couldn't bring myself to go home, I kept going, looping the path like I was burning something off. Fifteen thousand steps without realizing it.

Walking became my therapy. My escape.

I put my music on loud enough to drown out my thoughts. I listened to podcasts that reminded me that other people had gotten through worse. I half-heard speeches while my feet kept moving.

With my father safe under my daughter's care, I could disappear into motion. Sweat. Breath. Forward momentum.

That was the beginning.

Not a transformation. Not a miracle.

Just the first time I chose my body rather than abandoning it.

It wasn't just exercise.

It was training.

I was building the stamina to be gone from the house, from the center of gravity always pulling me in, and still enjoy myself. Testing whether I could leave other people in charge without unraveling. Teaching my nervous system that everything didn't have to be done exactly to spec to still be safe. If another caregiver knew the basics, my mind could loosen its grip. My father would be okay.

I didn't know it yet, but I was training myself to leave.

Not permanently.

Just long enough to remember who I was when nothing was actively falling apart.

So, when my bags were packed and the journey to Mexico began, it didn't feel reckless.

It felt earned.

I arrived at Sue's house with the giddy energy of a teenager sneaking out for the first time. We'd been talking about this trip for months. Sue had been one of my closest friends for years. She laughed hard, said yes to almost anything, and was always up for an adventure.

"I can't believe we're really doing this," I said, dropping my bag by the door.

"I know," Sue said, already smiling. "I've been counting down to the sun. Nin's on her way," she added. "She said ten minutes."

An hour later, the three of us reached our gate at the airport and sat, bags tucked under our feet, watching the boarding time tick down like it might change its mind. Getting there had been mercifully uneventful, which felt like its own small victory.

Finally, the announcement crackled over the loudspeaker.

"We will now begin boarding for Cabo San Lucas."

I felt it then. Excitement tangled with worry, adrenaline brushing up against relief. It was actually happening. I was about to spend my fiftieth birthday poolside with my best friends. Maybe meet some new ones. Step into the second half of my life somewhere warm, loud, and unapologetically alive.

When the plane lifted off, I felt something I hadn't felt in years: I wasn't responsible for whatever happened next.

I was sitting between Ninette and Sue. They never asked too many questions and never hesitated when someone said, "Let's do it." They knew the difference between when you need distraction and when you need tequila.

As the engines roared and the ground fell away, Nin leaned forward across our row, grinning. "We're really doing this."

Sue smiled, calm as always. "Of course we are."

Something in my chest loosened.

Not relief.

Permission.

We landed in Cabo, and the heat wrapped around us immediately. Thick and bright. Like the sun had been waiting. It didn't ask anything of me. No schedules. No alarms. No listening for footsteps in the night. Just warmth, noise, and movement.

Our days filled fast.

We rode camels along the beach, laughing as they groaned and swayed beneath us. I remember gripping the saddle, the ocean stretched wide beside us, wind in my face, thinking how absurd and perfect it felt to be doing something so unnecessary. Nin swore she would never get on a camel again. By the end, she was posing next to one, arms up like she'd conquered it.

We swam with dolphins. The trainer ran through the routine, then offered the option to dive with one. I raised my hand immediately. No hesitation. The trainer showed me how to hold the fins and counted us down.

"One. Two. Three. Hold your breath—"

And suddenly I was underwater, flying. I swear I heard *The Little Mermaid* soundtrack in my head as the dolphin carried me down and then shot us back up to the surface. Sue clapped from the edge of the pool. Nin yelled, "You're insane," laughing so hard she had to grab the rail.

Poolside afternoons were filled with frozen drinks and conversations that wandered wherever they wanted. Waiters appeared before we realized our glasses were empty. Sue would take a sip, tilt her head slightly, and say, "That's delicious."

It made me laugh every time.

Nin, on the other hand, would scan the scene, clock something ridiculous, and deliver a comment so sharp it left us crying-laughing. These friendships were tight—most female friendships are—and I couldn't imagine spending my birthday without Nin and Sue by my side.

There were foam parties with a DJ thumping in the background, bubbles clinging to our hair and sunburned shoulders.

At the start of our trip, Nin had sworn she would absolutely not participate. Two days later, she was waist-deep in foam, hands in the air, laughing as if she'd never said no in her life.

Later that afternoon, we collapsed into loungers, skin sticky with sunscreen and salt, hair still damp, the DJ fading into background noise. Someone dropped fresh towels across our legs. Sue stretched her feet toward the sun and sighed as if she'd just remembered how to breathe.

Nin leaned over toward me, lowering her voice like she was proposing something dangerous.

"We should book massages while we're here."

I laughed. "Obviously."

"No, I'm serious," she said, pushing her sunglasses up on her head. "We both need it."

She wasn't wrong. I could feel it everywhere. Not soreness exactly. More like my body had been holding its breath for years and didn't know how to exhale without permission.

"On the beach though," I said. "Not inside. I want waves and wind and zero walls."

Sue lifted her head. "If you're doing it, I'm doing it," she said. "But I'm warning you, if I fall asleep and snore, that's between me and God."

Nin grinned. "Perfect. That's how you know it's working."

"Tomorrow then," I said, and we clinked our half-melted drinks together like it was a contract.

The sun beaming early woke me, and I walked barefoot across the sand toward the cabana, the fabric panels lifting and falling with the breeze like they were breathing. The ocean stretched out behind it, endless and loud, waves crashing and retreating. Two massage therapists greeted me with warm smiles.

I climbed onto the table and let the sheets settle over me, light and cool against skin that had spent years braced, guarded, tight. The sound of the surf filled my ears, close enough that it felt like it was moving through me instead of around me. When their hands first pressed into my back, my body flinched without permission—a muscle memory of defense, of holding it together.

But they worked slowly. Patiently. Their fingers found knots I had stopped noticing because they had become permanent. My shoulders resisted. My neck pushed back. My lower back stayed rigid, unwilling to trust.

Then, inch by inch, something shifted.

Heat. Pressure. Release.

My shoulders dropped without me telling them to. My jaw loosened. My breath became fuller, moved lower, deeper, no longer stuck high in my chest like a never-ending alarm. The tension didn't vanish all at once. It unraveled. Thread by thread.

I lay there listening to the water, tasting salt in the air. Sun filtered through the cabana walls, and laughter drifted in from somewhere nearby. For the first time in years, my body wasn't on alert. It wasn't waiting for footsteps or listening for doors. It wasn't holding space for anyone else.

It was just mine.

Standing up afterward, sand still clinging to my feet, my skin warm and loose, I understood something: Freedom isn't loud. It doesn't announce itself. Sometimes it shows up in a body that finally stops fighting. In a moment where nothing is required. In the simple realization that we're allowed to want more than survival.

Chapter 20

One Eye Open

I came home with the perfect tan and the look of complete relaxation, carrying the faint, sweet smell of sunscreen that no shower quite removes. It clung to my skin like proof that I had been somewhere else. Somewhere warm. Somewhere where my body had been allowed to soften.

My bag hit the floor, still half-zipped, sand tucked into the seams.

Before I could bend to pick it up, my father saw me.

His whole face changed.

"Hey there! How ya doin?" he said, standing up too fast, reaching for me with both hands like I had been gone a year instead of a week.

I wrapped my arms around him and felt how light he'd gotten in just seven days. Or maybe I had just forgotten what holding him felt like. His shoulders seemed smaller. His frame easier to lift. The thought landed and stayed.

"You want to see what I did?" I asked, already pulling my phone from my pocket.

He sat down on the couch, pleased, expectant, leaning forward like a kid waiting for proof. I scrolled through my photos. There we were—the three of us laughing, hair everywhere, the ocean behind us, riding camels on the beach.

"You rode that thing?" he asked, pointing at the screen.

"I did."

He nodded, serious. "What's that called again?"

"It's a camel, Dad."

"Looks stubborn," he said, chuckling.

Then I showed him the dolphin video. The one where I dove. The one where I disappeared under the water, holding on, and came shooting back up, gasping and laughing.

He slapped his knee and laughed. "Wow," he said. "You're always doing something crazy."

He watched it again. And again. Like he was trying to store it somewhere safe. I stayed beside him longer than I needed to. Let him hold my hand. Neither of us rushed to move.

Caregiving has joy in it. Real joy. Not the Instagram kind. It lives in moments like these.

I knew I was lucky to love him this much at the end of his life. I knew not everyone gets that.

But joy has a curfew.

Because once it got dark, there was no escape.

My tan faded quickly under the weight of night. Whatever I had reset in Cabo burned off fast, like adrenaline after an emergency. My well-being took a back seat again—without discussion, without ceremony, without hardly a second thought. Sleep became negotiable. Energy became a rationed resource. I was back to full-body listening, tensed to hear the slightest movement.

The night I got back was the night the games got stealthier.

He had already been hoarding items we let slide. Spoons. Napkins. Pudding cups. Small disappearances that felt almost harmless. But this was different.

He started hiding EVERYTHING.

He'd take bananas from the kitchen and hide the peels instead of throwing them away. Under the couch. Behind furniture. In the corners of his room. Days later, I would find them, blackened and shriveled, curled in on themselves like secrets. The smell always hit first. Sweet. Rotten. Wrong.

I never saw him take them. Never caught him in the act. He moved when no one was looking.

We started calling him the Banana Bandit because if I didn't laugh, I would have cried.

We locked the cabinets. Covered the fruit. Rearranged the kitchen like a puzzle meant to outsmart someone who no longer played by the rules. And still, somehow, he found them.

"Which game are we playing today?" Bri asked one morning, standing in the kitchen in her socks, coffee in hand.

I smiled too quickly. "Depends what we find."

She laughed. I exhaled. Laughter bought us seconds.

The sun-downing had started months before, but this time it was different. He was on medications that should have knocked out a horse, but still, he would wake up. It seemed that no amount of medication could contain the restless confusion that had taken over his mind. Pills lined up like soldiers. Names I couldn't pronounce. Doses I checked and double-checked.

And still, he woke.

Over and over.

Wandering. Opening doors. Standing in the hallway like he was waiting for instructions that no one could give him. Trying to leave.

I stopped sleeping in full stretches. Even when my eyes closed, my body stayed on. Listening. Counting footsteps. Waiting for the sound of a door opening where it shouldn't.

He had figured out every lock we had put on the doors. Once he did, he'd slip outside trying to find home.

It was Collin who finally cracked it.

"Mom," he said one afternoon, leaning against the counter. "He might have figured out all the locks. But why don't you just lock the front storm door?"

It was so simple I felt ridiculous.

That night, I locked it.

I watched him try.

Watched the handle turn. Watched the pause. Watched frustration ripple across his face.

"It's broken," I told him, steady, casual, like it had always been that way.

He looked at it again. Tugged once more. Then nodded.

"Oh," he said. "Okay."

And he walked away.

I put on *Gunsmoke*. Handed him pudding. We managed through another night.

He had no sense of time. No understanding that it was dark or that morning was still hours away. Night stretched endlessly, without edges.

I slept in pieces.

I slept sitting up.

I slept listening.

Every sound came through my body before my brain could catch up. The creak of a floorboard. The whisper of fabric. A door shifting on its hinge.

My nervous system never powered down.

By morning, my jaw ached from clenching. My shoulders burned. My thoughts moved more slowly, like they had to push through something thick before forming.

I started to worry about what would happen if I missed something. If I slept too deeply. If my reaction time lagged by seconds, that mattered.

I watched him like a hawk.

And hawks don't rest.

They hover.

They scan.

They survive by not blinking.

By the time daylight came, I was already empty. Not emotionally. Physically. Like my body had spent something it could not regenerate.

I stood in the kitchen, coffee growing cold in my hand, and realized something quietly, without drama, without panic:

This is not sustainable.

Chapter 21

The Body Gives Way

The mornings came and went, each one passing quickly while my body continued its own form of shutdown. Nothing dramatic. Just depletion. I was running on fumes and momentum, and even that was thinning.

I heard the front door open at eight on the dot.

Brianna.

Relief landed immediately, physical and undeniable.

She came in with a Dunkin' Donuts cup in her hand, her short, tight curls neat and close to her head, already awake in a way I was not.

"How's it going?" she asked.

"I'm good," I said automatically, then stopped. "Actually, I'm not. I'm really glad you're here. I need a nap."

She nodded. "Is he up?"

"I don't know," I said. "Let's go check."

We walked upstairs to find him.

The bathroom door was open.

He stood in front of the toilet, unmoving. Not sitting. Not going. Just staring down, like he was waiting for his body to remember something it no longer knew how to do.

His incontinence had begun to get worse, so he was wearing underwear designed to hold small amounts of urine.

But his underwear was on the floor, feet from where he was standing.

Brianna spotted them first. She picked them up and froze.

"Mom," she said, shocked. "This looks like blood."

My stomach dropped.

"Holy shit."

I didn't know where it was coming from, and that terrified me more than knowing.

He had come home from his initial discharge with a catheter, a standard one placed through his urethra, but they had removed it to see if he could manage on his own. The doctor wanted to monitor him, to give his body a chance. I already knew the answer.

I called the doctor immediately and got him a 9:30 AM appointment.

They took him straight back and got an ultrasound of his bladder.

It was massive. Swollen far beyond normal, stretched to a size that made my chest tighten just looking at it.

The doctor pointed to the screen. "His brain isn't signaling his bladder to empty anymore," he said. "He has a severe bladder infection."

I nodded, steady on the outside.

"He'll need antibiotics," he continued. "And surgery."

Surgery.

For the first time in his life.

He would be getting a supra-pubic catheter.

A permanent one.

What followed that surgery was absolute hell.

Try explaining to someone with dementia that they now have a tube inserted through a small opening in their lower abdomen, just above the pubic bone, that drains urine directly from their bladder.

Try explaining bodily loss to a mind that cannot hold cause and effect.

The tube itself didn't bother him. He rarely noticed it. It sat there quietly, a small opening in his stomach that had to be cleaned every day, carefully and methodically. I cleaned the site. I checked for redness. I watched for infection. I learned the rules. The bag always had to stay below bladder level. The system had to remain intact.

What he couldn't tolerate was the bag.

The plastic. The weight. The foreignness of it hanging there.

"What's that?" he asked the first time he noticed it.

"That helps your body do what it needs to do," I said.

He frowned. "I don't need it."

"I know," I said, because arguing never worked.

He didn't touch the tube. Never pulled at it. Some part of him understood that it was now part of his body.

But the bag?

That was negotiable.

In the days after surgery, I thought we had gotten acquainted with this new equipment and adjusted. He was compliant, even curious, when I cleaned the insertion site or emptied the bag. He watched my hands closely, like he was trying to memorize the steps.

"What are you doing?" he would ask.

"Taking care of the incision site. I will make it quick."

"Oh," he'd say, satisfied for the moment.

But as more time passed, his curiosity vanished.

One afternoon, about a week after his surgery, Bri was downstairs making his lunch while I sat in my office, laptop open, trying to keep my business alive. I saw movement out of the corner of my eye.

He was coming down the stairs.

"Hi, Than," he said, waving.

He had on a pair of aviator sunglasses that he must have taken from Darius's car. They made him look ridiculous and confident at the same time.

"Hi, Dad," I said. "Time for lunch?"

"Yup," he said. "I'm gonna go see if the guys are in the . . . place over there."

The prison. His old work life resurfacing.

"Okay," I said. "Let me know what's for lunch."

Then I saw it.

A thin, glistening line across the carpet.

My heart slammed.

I stood up fast.

"No. No. No," I said. "Dad. Stop."

He looked down, confused.

"What?"

The bag was gone.

Not the tube.

The bag.

Somehow, quietly, instinctively, he had disconnected it and discarded it like it didn't belong to him.

"Where's the bag?" I asked.

He shrugged. "Didn't need it."

Every part of my body went hot. This was not going away.

After that, the bag disappeared daily.

I'd find it under the bed. Under his pillow. Stuffed behind furniture. Once I found it tucked inside a laundry basket like it had always lived there.

This wasn't hoarding. This was flat-out rejection.

And it was dangerous.

We started checking the usual places like detectives.

"Look under his pillow," I'd say.

Bri would already be moving. "Got it."

Sometimes we found it quickly. Sometimes we didn't. Every time it vanished, my chest tightened. Infection risk. Spillage. Exposure. The system only worked if every piece stayed where it belonged.

So, I adapted.

Again.

Like the storm door locks, like the cabinet locks, I found another workaround. Another solution. Another move in a game I didn't want to play.

I found catheter socks on Amazon. Soft cloth sleeves that pulled onto his leg like a sock and held the bag snug against his upper thigh, hidden under his clothing. It was less visible that way. Less accessible. Less plastic against his skin.

He tolerated those better.

They were warmer. More human.

And still, I felt like I was losing.

Bathing became another negotiation.

And then it became a risk.

Every time we helped him shower, I held my breath as he lifted his foot over the threshold. If he slipped, he'd take me with him.

That's when it became clear that caring for him wasn't just about keeping him safe anymore.

I had to keep myself safe, too.

Around that time, we moved him to a downstairs bedroom, close enough that we could hear him move. Close enough to preempt wherever he decided to go. But even that change wasn't enough. The bathroom needed to be fixed.

We remodeled. Removed barriers. Planned for what we didn't want to name.

Diego handled the construction. We had known each other for years from my time in finance, and by then, he felt more like family than a contractor.

I designed every inch of that bathroom with aging in mind—walk-in access, wider clearance, grab bars that didn't scream hospital. We fought like siblings over finishes and functionality until we landed on both—safe enough for my father, beautiful enough that it didn't feel like we were surrendering our home to illness.

The house stopped being a home.

It became a system.

And without ceremony, without a single clean moment of realization, something shifted.

I wasn't preparing anymore.

I was responding.

I wasn't watching caregiving happen.

I was fully living inside it.

And every day felt like cat and mouse.

Every day, I felt one step behind.

I kept chasing routines that never lasted. His disease moved faster than any system I built.

One night, I was getting him ready for bed, working through our usual process. Pajamas laid out. Lights lowered. The bag emptied and reattached carefully. Fabric rustled as I pulled the catheter sock back into place under his pants. I narrated just enough to keep him from spiraling.

"Okay," I said. "Arms up."

He did. Then hesitated.

"What are we doing?" he asked.

"Getting ready for bed."

He looked at the pajamas in my hands like he'd never seen them before.

"Whose room is this?"

"Yours," I said gently.

He nodded, then frowned. "I gotta go home."

"You are home."

He glanced around again. The bed. The dresser. The lamp we'd moved downstairs. His face tightened, not angry, just uncertain.

"Well," he said, "I don't want to be late."

"Late for what?"

He opened his mouth, then closed it. Thought about it. Shook his head slightly.

"They'll be looking for me," he said.

"Who will?"

He studied my face like the answer might be written there. "The guys."

I felt it then. Sharp and immediate.

"You're off tonight," I said. "You worked all day."

He relaxed a little at that. "I did?"

"You did."

He let me help him sit on the edge of the bed. I pulled the pajama top over his head. He caught his arm in the sleeve and laughed softly, embarrassed.

"I'm not very good at this anymore," he said.

"I've got you," I said.

He looked up at me, suddenly serious. "Are you my nurse?"

The question wasn't accusing. Just curious.

I swallowed. "I'm your daughter."

He searched my face again. "Huh."

Then, after a moment, "You look familiar."

It landed like a punch to my gut.

Things are different now.

Something deep inside me knew these may be some of the last times he truly remembered his family. The last time he understood what Christmas was. The last time the season meant anything to him beyond lights and noise.

His confusion was growing.

He didn't always recognize my mother anymore.

And Brianna, who cared for him alongside me every day, who knew his routines, his moods, his tells, who had celebrated him year after year in the backyard with cake and laughter and candles, became someone else in his mind entirely.

He started mistaking her for a security guard at the prison.

He would look at her with suspicion. With fear. As if she were one of the "people" assigned to keep him there.

Watching that happen felt like a quiet betrayal of reality itself. The person who fed him, bathed him, protected him, sat with him through confusion and frustration was suddenly recast as a threat.

Every day, every night, I watched as pieces of the brilliant man I knew disappeared. It was brutal to witness; I remembered exactly who he was—who he had been.

I remembered the man who read for hours. The sharp, intelligent mind that could take apart an idea and rebuild it better. The way he solved problems confidently.

I remembered the father who taught me how to drive a truck. Who drilled independence into me. Who made it clear that no one ever got to decide my limits but me.

I also remembered the earlier fractures. The confusion long before anyone named it. The years I spent advocating, protecting, and translating his reality to others while still trying to be his daughter.

Still, I never lost sight of the gratitude.

Because even as he disappeared, I still had him.

I could still hold his hand. I could still hear his voice. I could still sit beside him and remind him, if only for a moment, that he was safe. That he was loved.

And no matter how painful it was to watch, I would not trade those moments for anything.

I was grateful that I had the ability, the means, and the space to care for him in my home. Grateful that I could say goodbye slowly. That I could hold onto every moment, even the ones that hurt.

He was disappearing.

And I had a front-row seat.

There was nothing I could do to stop it.

Chapter 22

Winter Wonderland

By the time Christmas arrived, the house belonged to the season.

Every room held it. White, gold, and silver caught the light at every turn, and our house, purchased exactly for this purpose, shimmered.

I didn't want subtlety. I didn't want suggestion. I wanted immersion. Garland draped along stair rails and doorframes. Ornaments tucked everywhere. All three bathrooms featured Christmas in miniature, small trees on counters, hand towels stitched with snowflakes, candles that smelled like pine and sugar.

I bought five live trees first. Then ten more artificial ones. Different sizes and shapes for every room, all of them lit and glowing.

It looked like winter had lost control inside our house. Like Christmas had arrived and refused to leave. The sweet scent of pine permeated every room.

Soon, the house was packed with family.

Every room was filled. Voices overlapping. Laughter bouncing off walls. Coats hung in the front closet like a hotel lobby coat check. Shoes lined up in imperfect rows near the door. The kitchen ran hot, stovetop crowded, the smell of roasting meat and butter and sugar thick in the air.

People who loved my father were everywhere you turned.

I watched him move through it all slowly, carefully. Hands brushing the backs of chairs. Fingers grazing garland. Pausing in doorways as if the house itself was asking him to stop and notice.

I wanted this Christmas to register in his body, even if his mind couldn't hold all the details.

I wanted something unmistakably familiar and safe.

Something that said: You are surrounded. You are home. You matter.

The meal was a feast.

Prime rib sliced thick and pink. Popovers tearing open with steam. Green bean casserole bubbling at the edges. Sweet potatoes glazed and soft. Mashed potatoes piled high. Broccoli casserole browned just enough on top.

Plates heavy. Tables full.

People lingered. No one rushed. Forks rested midair as conversations took over.

I watched him, barely noticing how I still noticed everything about his movements, his orbit, even with the house full and others looking out for him.

Brianna refilled his water. Collin pulled out a chair before he even asked.

He sat at the table longer than usual, listening more than speaking, eyes moving from face to face.

"Good food," he said quietly at one point, nodding.

"It is," I said.

He smiled at that.

After dinner, the crowd migrated downstairs.

The man cave filled the way the rest of the house had. Bodies settling into couches and chairs, people standing along the walls, drinks balanced on knees and side tables. Wrapping paper already piled in the corner. Angel turned on music low enough to talk over.

This was where we gathered every year. Where birthdays were celebrated. Where football games played in the background, whether anyone watched or not. Familiar ground.

We circled up for gifts.

It was time for White Elephant, another tradition.

Numbers got passed around to each participant. The gifts, piled high on the table near the bar, dwindled as we cycled through. Haley kept trying to peek at unopened boxes. Jamie, my sister's fiancé, circled the room like he was scouting weak targets. Nadene was already laughing before the game even got competitive.

"Absolutely not," Brianna said, clutching a gift tighter as hands reached for it.

"That's not fair," Jamie laughed. "You already stole twice."

"I waited my whole life for this moment," Collin said, reaching for the same bag again.

The Yeti mug became the prize.

It bounced from lap to lap—stolen, reclaimed, fought over like it was worth far more than it was. Diego finally got his hands on it and lifted it over his head like he'd won the lottery. Thirty seconds later, Haley stole it right back.

"Come on!"

"You've got to be kidding me!"

"That's cold."

My father sat back in his chair, hands folded loosely in his lap.

He watched it all.

His eyes tracked the movement of the gift. The hands. The laughter. He didn't reach for anything. Didn't protest. Just observed, head turning slightly as the mug changed owners again.

At one point, when Collin finally lost it for good, my father let out a short laugh. Surprised himself with it.

"Well," he said, shaking his head, smiling, "guess that's settled."

The room quieted for half a second, then laughed again.

My mother handed him a small gift of his own. He turned it over slowly, examining the paper before opening it carefully. When he finished, he looked up.

"Thank you," he said, sincere, warm.

He didn't say who he was thanking.

But it didn't matter.

The noise rose and fell. Darius told a story I'd heard before. Diego reached for another drink. Wrapping paper crinkled underfoot.

And my father sat there the entire time, smiling.

Sometimes he leaned forward when the laughter got loud. Sometimes he closed his eyes for a moment, not sleeping, just resting inside the sound. Sometimes he chimed in with a comment that fit just enough to make everyone laugh again.

I watched him from across the room.

"How ya doin dad?"

"The best I can with what I got." It was a response he echoed often. I chuckled and wondered if he knew exactly who was there.

If he could name everyone.

If that even mattered.

Because when I looked at him, I saw contentment. Ease. A body at rest inside a room full of people who loved him.

He wasn't searching. He wasn't agitated. He wasn't afraid.

He was present.

That was the gift.

That Christmas, Christmas 2022, wasn't about tradition or perfection or memory-making.

It was about presence.

It was about love made visible.

It was for him.

And it was beautiful.

Chapter 23

My Tribe

Going to Cabo to celebrate my fiftieth was the test of whether or not our caregiving systems would hold, and in 2023, I had the proof.

The systems held. The routines did what they were designed to do. I was able to leave the house. I traveled. I showed up at events. I filled the calendar and kept things moving. I built a structure around us and, inside it, we functioned. Dad was cared for. The house ran. Life continued, at least on the surface.

I told myself this was what adaptation looked like. I believed it.

In a group text with five of my friends from high school—all of us still thick as thieves, Michelle suggested a weekend together. Wine and shenanigans were implied. Everyone knew it would be easiest at my house. I had the space. The bedrooms. The bar.

And so they arrived, one by one, in the cold February air. Each of them brought wine. Not a bottle. Bottles. It felt intentional. Necessary.

By nightfall, the house was full again.

My neighbor Kate stopped by. My son's girlfriend, Angel, joined. Music got louder. Imani started dancing in the kitchen while Ninette hyped her up from the island. It turned into something that felt like a teenage sleepover, just louder, and instead of Bartles & James, it was bougie Pinot and Chardonnay.

The music lowered eventually. Not off. Just low enough that conversations could stretch without shouting. We settled into couches and chairs, refilled our wine glasses, and kicked off our shoes.

The night softened, at least for a moment.

With our glasses emptied, I got up and went to the bar. No announcement. No question. Just instinct.

The tequila came out first. Then the limes. Salt already smudged the edge of a plate. I made our margaritas and shook them the way I always do, strong enough to matter.

Ninette watched me closely, hands folded, posture polite, as if she were observing a major crime.

"Okay," she said carefully, "I just want to say, for the record, that margaritas are a *choice*."

I slid her the glass. "You can handle it."

She took a sip. Paused. Took another, longer one.

"Oh," she said, blinking. "Well. That escalated quickly."

Michelle laughed. "She's gone."

"I am not *gone*," Ninette said, clutching the glass. "I'm just . . . recalibrating."

I poured again without asking.

"I just need everyone to understand," Ninette continued, already warmer, "that if I say something deeply inappropriate tonight, tequila started it."

"Tequila always does," I said.

Lisette had already drifted toward the back door with Kim, rosé in one hand, a lighter in the other. "We'll be outside," she smiled. "For . . . fresh air."

The door slid shut behind them. Laughter leaked through the glass.

Later, the tequila gave way to wine again. More bottles opened. More glasses filled and refilled. The night stretched into itself the way it always does when no one's counting hours.

Ninette sat cross-legged on the floor, her back against the recliner, looking at me over the rim of her glass.

"So," she said gently. "How's your dad really doing?"

The room didn't go silent, but it shifted. Everyone knew this question. Everyone knew better than to rush it.

"He's okay," I said. "I mean . . . he's stable. The systems are working."

Kim nodded slowly, the way she always did when she was listening closely. "And you?"

I opened my mouth, then closed it. Laughed a little.

"I'm functioning," I said.

Lisette, who had been living with us and knew the rhythms of the house better than anyone, reached over and squeezed my foot. "That's not what she asked."

Michelle leaned forward. "You don't have to be brave in here."

Kate glanced toward the hallway, then back at me. "He seems happy tonight. He really does."

"He is," I said. "The noise helps. He likes knowing people are around."

Imani sat on the arm of the chair watching me, quiet but present, holding space without needing to fill it.

"You don't ever have to explain it," she said. "We see you."

Angel had been curled up on the other end of the couch, listening more than talking. She smiled at me, soft and earnest.

"You're doing a really good job," she said. "Like . . . really good."

I shook my head. "I operate on autopilot half the time. I'm not gonna lie—I'm tired, frustrated—but like my dad always says, 'I'm doin the best I can with what I got.'"

Ninette snorted. "That line should be embroidered on your life."

Laughter rippled through the room, easy and familiar.

Kim raised her glass. "To showing up anyway."

We clinked, not ceremoniously, just enough to mark the moment.

No one offered advice. No one tried to fix anything. They simply asked. They listened. They stayed.

That mattered more than I could explain.

Darius stayed with Dad that night. They sat in the family room just outside the man cave we had claimed. Dad sat in his chair, content in the noise. Our laughter carried through the house, and he followed it like background music.

"You good?" he asked us, peeking into the room.

"We're good, Dad," I said.

"Fast Eddie, you wanna join us?" Ninette called out, grinning, gesturing toward the chaos.

"Nah, nah," he said, waving his hand. "You girls are too much for me. I'm going to bed. Good to see ya."

He turned and, just like that, Darius was at his side, guiding him upstairs.

The next morning, we moved slowly. We ate a light breakfast of toast and coffee. Whatever would absorb the night before. We lingered at the counter, replaying old stories, already trying to plan the next weekend like this one.

Then, the way it always happens, they left. One by one, we hugged at the door, then their cars pulled away.

Afterward, I stood at the counter wiping rings from the granite, the dishwasher groaning to life beside me. Angel gathered abandoned wine glasses while Darius took out the trash. Our noise slowly drained out of the rooms. The house settled back into itself.

It felt normal.

Earned.

Like proof that caregiving had not swallowed me whole.

That he could still laugh. Still respond.

And that mattered.

Chapter 24

Bearing Weight

Spring came without urgency.

Not all at once. Not with a shift you could point to. It crept in through longer light at the kitchen window, through days that no longer felt pressed for time. We all had become accustomed to a steadier pace, one that didn't demand constant correction.

I had promised Mom, when she moved up, that we would plant a garden with Dad. It would be something to give the days a shape. Something that pointed forward instead of folding back in on itself. And it was time to begin.

We started at the kitchen table, seed packets spread everywhere, tomatoes, basil, peppers, and cucumbers scattered between us like tiny promises. Dirt worked its way under our nails before we planted anything in the ground.

Dad picked up each envelope carefully, turning it over like it might change if he looked long enough.

"These are tomatoes?"

"Yup."

He nodded, studied another packet, then looked up.

"And these?"

I smiled. "Tomatoes."

We did this more than once. The same questions. The same answers. I learned not to rush it. Learned that the pace mattered more than progress.

Outside, Darius and I started on the raised beds. The ground was still damp from winter, soft in places that hadn't seen the sun yet. We measured twice. Cut once. Then measured again anyway. I played YouTube tutorials on my phone, paused them to make a measurement, went back thirty seconds, then paused again, until the cuts finally lined up. Sawdust clung to our clothes. Mud collected on the soles of our shoes.

We worked side by side without much talking at first. Tools passed back and forth. Screws dropped and retrieved. We found a groove that didn't need narration.

"Can you hold that for me?" he asked, bracing one end while I lined up the drill.

"Got it," I said.

Our hands brushed when we switched places. Neither of us commented on it. It felt like we were doing something together, not just occupying the same space.

When the first bed finally took shape, we stepped back, hands on our hips, looking at it.

"Looks good," he said.

"I know, right? Told you we could do it."

It wasn't really about the garden. The garden was proof. It was something solid we could stand in front of and say we made this. Something that suggested continuity. Partnership.

After that, our days fell back into repetition. Morning routines. Meals. Medications. The same loops running cleanly. Care folded into the day without tearing it open. I left the house. I came back. Nothing unraveled while I was gone.

There were moments when I realized I could take care of him and still have a life. I had built a foundation. A structure that leaned on friends, family, and whatever systems could be bent into service. I stayed alert, always, but I could function inside the boundaries I'd built to keep him safe.

One evening, all of us in the family room watching TV, I was scrolling through Facebook without thinking when a post stopped me.

"Five hundred dollars. You can get one of these guys for less than a mortgage payment," it read.

In the picture, along with it, one of my friends stood smiling, two black Labradoodle puppies tucked under his arms.

My mind went there immediately. We had lost our dog Creed months earlier, and the absence he left behind still pressed in at odd moments. *Lola could use a friend,* I thought. *Another brother.*

I showed the picture to Darius.

"No," he said. It was immediate. Flat.

He didn't share my attachment to animals. He never had.

A few days later, I went to the breeder anyway.

I sat down, and one puppy with a little green collar climbed straight into my lap while his eight siblings tore around the room. None of them had names, so the breeder referred to them by the colors on their collars.

The pink one gnawed at my shoes.

The yellow and the blue tried to scale my back, while the purple attempted to eat my watch.

The green one didn't move. He curled in, pressed his weight into me, and stayed.

That was it. He stole my heart.

I looked up at the breeder. "Finley," I said, nodding at the puppy in my lap. "He looks like a Finley." My mind was made up, not just my heart. "He's the one," I said, definitively.

Days later, he arrived with too much energy and no understanding of personal space. A black whirlwind with legs that moved faster than his judgment. Lola watched from her spot like a seasoned supervisor, unimpressed but curious.

Finley skidded across the floor, slid into the wall, and popped up as if nothing had happened.

Dad laughed.

"That dog's got no brakes."

"I know, right? He's so cute. He's gonna be a big boy."

Lola corrected him when she needed to. Followed him from room to room, just close enough to keep an eye on things. The house absorbed it all. The noise. The movement. The small chaos of a puppy.

Dad stayed present. Content to watch it happen around him. Every so often, a flicker of joy crossed his face as the two dogs chased each other through the rooms.

Morning came, and Bri arrived with coffee in hand, already moving like she knew the day's weight.

"What've you got going on today?" she asked.

"I've got a few client calls, then me and Papa are heading out for his birthday dinner."

"You look nice," she said, approving.

"Thanks. I figured I'd put in a little effort. It's his birthday."

I shot her a wink.

She gave that Brianna chuckle and headed into the kitchen, where Dad was working through breakfast. Upstairs, I could hear Diego moving around the bathroom, tools hitting tile in uneven bursts. Darius was getting dressed for dinner.

I took each call without interruption, watching sunlight catch on the grass outside, still shimmering from the heavy rain the night before.

"C'mon, Finley, let's go for a run," I said when I'd finished for the day. I was just as excited as he was to get out; I needed to feel the sun on my skin.

I clipped the long lead onto his collar.

He took off the way he always did, puppy energy burning through him. I let him run a little. Then he bolted, and I reacted without thinking, stepping on the leash and forgetting entirely about last night's rain.

It was like slow motion—my right leg slipping underneath me, my left leg planted in nothing but mud.

I heard the snap and the crack.

"FUCK FUCK FUCK," I screamed at the top of my lungs, praying someone would hear me.

Then the pain hit, sharp and immediate, dragging tears with it.

Brianna rushed around the corner, seeing me and my white linen pants now full of mud, the tears streaming down my face.

"Call 911," I told her, nearly hysterical. "I broke it, I know I did!"

"Oh my God, Mom, what happened?" she asked, her fingers punching in the numbers.

"Take him," I said, handing her Finley's leash that I was somehow still gripping onto. "I slipped in the mud. Call Aunt Deenie, tell her she needs to come NOW."

The EMTs arrived with their lights and questions, their hands steadying me as they lifted me onto the stretcher.

At the hospital, I lay in a bed with the rails up, my leg already swelling, wrapped and immobilized. Darius sat beside me, his birthday ticking past us under fluorescent lights. Honey-roasted peanuts from a vending machine sat on the tray between us. Nothing else was edible.

They had drugged me enough that standing wasn't an option.

"So sorry this happened," I said to Darius. "I was looking forward to a nice dinner."

"It's okay," he consoled me. "It wasn't your fault; these things happen."

Neither of us said what sat there between us.

Finley had been my idea.

After we put Creed down, the house felt different.

I had wanted something to bring the house back to life. Something that filled the space again.

Darius had never wanted another dog. We still had Lola. To him, that was enough.

He didn't say it.

But I knew.

I knew the way he held it in.

The way he always did.

Letting it sit there instead of pushing back.

I could feel it between us.

Not loud.

Not spoken.

But there all the same.

The nurse entered. "Time for some more pain meds and then off to X-ray."

She gave me a shot of something, and I felt my body fade into sleep. Before I knew it, I was in bed overnight with a huge cast wrapped around my leg. I had broken it in two places.

How am I going to manage Dad now? was my first thought.

Darius walked in, seeing I was awake. "They want to keep you here overnight," he confirmed. "Don't worry," he added quickly, "Nadene is here, and we will handle everything at home."

"And Dad?"

"He's fine. Bri stayed with him all day until your sister got here. I am going to head home and get things settled. You just rest. I will be back here tomorrow for discharge."

There was nothing else I could do. I was forced to stop. Stop thinking, stop doing. I had no choice but to allow others to care for me. There was nothing left to manage. No contingency to run through. No mental checklist looping in the background.

I lay back against the pillow while a nurse checked my vitals, the weight of the cast anchoring me to the bed.

The house was running.

Dad was safe.

Care was covered.

I could let myself rest.

The routines would hold without me standing inside them.

I had built it that way on purpose.

I had known the system wouldn't collapse, but so often I couldn't let myself believe it, wouldn't let myself put any extra weight on it for fear of it failing. Or maybe because I'd become so used to walking out every detail myself. Now I had to fall back and let the routines play out as designed—without me.

Chapter 25

Fast Eddie, R.N

I came home in a wheelchair. The break required surgery, a rod in place to hold the bone together.

Darius and Collin lifted me onto the front step while the dogs lost their minds behind the front door. When it opened, I smelled takeout—pizza, wings, something fried—mixed with the familiar scent of home.

Dad was waiting in his chair.

He watched the wheels roll in, his eyes tracking the cast first, then my face. He leaned forward, hands braced on the arms of the chair like he was about to stand, then stopped himself.

"Well, look at you," he said, concerned. "What'd you do?"

"I fell, Dad. They had to put a rod in my leg," I said.

He nodded once, absorbing it. Then his posture changed. It was subtle and unmistakable. His shoulders squared. His focus narrowed.

"Okay," he said. "You in pain?"

"Not bad," I said. "They've got me pretty numb."

"Good," he said. "That'll wear off."

He pointed at the cast.

"That's a mess."

"I know."

He didn't laugh. He assessed.

"Leg elevated," he said. "You gotta keep it iced when you can. Don't let it swell too much."

"I won't, but I may need your help."

"I'll help ya."

He looked past me, already scanning the room.

"Where's her pills?"

Lisette answered from the kitchen without missing a beat.

"On the counter, Fast Eddie. I have them ready for her."

Dad nodded. Satisfied.

That part of him, the R.N., never left.

The rest of the house moved like it had rehearsed.

Kate appeared with a tray and set it down beside me without asking. Soup. Crackers. Water with a straw.

"Text me if you need anything," she said. "I mean it."

"I know, and I really appreciate you. Thanks."

She nodded toward the back door. "I've got Finley. Morning and night. Don't even think about it."

I hadn't asked. I appreciated the assumption. The ownership.

She squeezed my shoulder and disappeared as quietly as she'd arrived.

Lisette stayed close. She knew the routines; she read the room. She moved things into reach. Anticipated what I needed and could sense when I was too tired to remember what mattered.

Darius handled the housework. Laundry folded. Groceries restocked. Dinners made, and the house kept clean.

Nadene rotated in and out, filling gaps without commentary on the weekends when she could. Follow-up appointments for dad. A break for Bri and Darius.

Someone always seemed to be arriving just as someone else left.

And Brianna stayed.

She helped me into bed that first night, lifting my leg to help me get comfortable. Adjusting pillows. Making sure the cast didn't press wrong.

"You good?" she asked.

"I am," I said.

She didn't leave right away. She sat on the edge of the bed, phone in her lap.

Dad appeared in the doorway not long after.

He stood there for a second, watching me, then stepped in.

"You need anything?" he asked.

"I'm okay," I said.

He didn't move.

"You sure?"

"I'm sure."

He nodded, satisfied enough to accept it. Then his eyes drifted back to the cast.

"What happened there?"

"I fell. I broke it."

He paused.

"That's no good."

"Nope."

He turned to Brianna.

"She's gotta keep that leg up."

"I know," she said.

"And don't let her rush it."

"I won't Gramps, but I may need your help. You're the nurse, not me."

"You got that right." He chuckled and restated, "I'll keep an eye on her."

That night, and many nights after, he checked on me the same way. No emotion. No panic. Just care. He would ask the same questions. Offer the same instructions. Each time like it was the first.

It kept him oriented. It gave him purpose.

I was off my feet for months.

Learning how to move again was slow and unglamorous. Crutches bruised my hands. The walker rattled. Every step required thought. Balance was something I had to negotiate instead of assume.

Dad watched it all.

"Slow," he'd say. "You're rushing."

"I'm okay," I'd assure him.

He'd tilt his head.

"You are."

And he was usually right.

Neighbors checked in. Friends stopped by. Meals arrived without explanation. Rides were offered. Errands handled. The house stayed upright.

Care flowed outward instead of collapsing inward.

And through it all, Fast Eddie stayed on duty.

Not as my father.

As my nurse.

He reminded me to take my meds. Asked about my pain levels. Watched my gait like it told him a story. Corrected my posture. Made sure I iced to avoid too much swelling.

His mind drifted elsewhere at times. Conversations looped. Names slipped.

But when it came to care, he was exact.

Present.

Reliable.

I had built the system for him.

And when I needed it, it held me too.

Chapter 26

The Prison of Care

Cold woke me before the alarm.

I went downstairs and checked the thermostat. Sixty-two. A number that meant the house hadn't caught up to the one degree day outside. I turned it up anyway and waited for the delayed click from the basement, the small mechanical confirmation that more heat was on its way.

By the time I stepped into the kitchen, my father was already there.

He sat at the table in his chair, hands folded, waiting. Not restless. Just ready, like the day had started without anyone consulting him.

"Can I get some coffee?" he asked.

"Sure can. I'm making it now."

The smell filled the room as I poured.

"Bri will be here soon," I said. "You guys can watch *Gunsmoke*. Or *Gilligan's Island*. Whatever you want."

"Okay."

"How you doing?"

"Best I can with what I got."

I smiled as I stirred his morning meds into his yogurt cup.

"That's all any of us can do, I suppose."

I slid the yogurt in front of him. He pushed it back immediately.

"I don't want that. What is it?"

"Your yogurt. Blueberry. Your favorite."

"I'll just drink my coffee."

I took the cup, let him sip, then placed it back in front of him.

"Here you go," I said lightly. "Blueberry."

I waited.

After a moment, he complied. Spoon dipped. A pause. Then another bite.

I exhaled without meaning to.

Food was never just food anymore. It was leverage. Timing. Strategy. Something I planned before I spoke.

"What about eggs?"

No.

"Soup?"

No.

Eventually, I stopped guessing.

Peanut butter and jelly almost always worked.

I set the plate down and waited.

"That's all?" he'd ask, suspicious.

"That's it. Just try."

Sometimes he'd finish it. Sometimes he didn't. But peanut butter and jelly kept him going, and that became the goal. Not a balanced diet, not variety. Calories. Something in his system was better than nothing.

There was no more leaving him in front of the TV while I stepped outside for a minute. No buffer. Every part of the day depended on someone being there.

His body was failing in quieter ways too. Diapers. Bathing. Dressing. Each step narrated so he wouldn't feel startled or ashamed.

"Lean forward."

"Hold the bar."

"I've got you."

He followed my lead without argument, trusting me completely.

Sleep stopped feeling like rest.

My hypervigilance deepened. I would shut my eyes, but my mind stayed open. Tracking sounds. Replaying the day. Anticipating the next need. Wine quieted things just enough to take the edge off. Not escape. Just pause.

At night, the house changed from a home into surveillance.

The rooms looked the same, but the rules didn't. Light emanated from screens instead of lamps. The ceiling glowed pale blue from the camera monitor. My body knew the hair-splitting difference between normal movement and something that meant I needed to move.

One night, I woke before I heard anything.

I checked the screen.

His bed was empty.

My feet hit the floor before my brain caught up. The hallway was cold. My heart was loud enough that I was sure it would wake the house. I found him halfway down the hall, confused, barefoot, turning in small circles like he was trying to remember why he'd stood up in the first place.

"Hey," I said, keeping my voice steady. "Where you headed?"

"I gotta go," he said. "I'm late."

"It's okay," I said. "Come back to bed."

He hesitated.

I stepped closer and took his arm.

"We'll go in the morning."

That night, and the nights that followed, played out in variations. Different rooms. Different reasons. Same ending.

My fear sharpened.

Not of the wandering itself, but of what it could turn into if I missed him by a minute, if his bare feet took him to a stairwell. I started to imagine the sound. A dull thud somewhere in the house. A pause that lasted too long. Silence where there shouldn't be silence. I pictured myself running across cold floors, rounding the corner to the stairs, and finding him crumpled at the bottom, broken in a way I could not undo.

I had cameras. Eyes on him almost everywhere. And still, he found ways to disappear.

The house rearranged itself in the dark. Corners became hiding places. Blind spots stretched. Rooms took on edges I didn't recognize during the day. I would scan the screen, then move, checking one space and then another, my heart climbing every time I didn't see him where he should have been. It felt less like caregiving and more like a game I could never win, except the cost of losing was not negotiable.

I stopped sleeping altogether, waiting for daylight.

I learned how long I could lie still before I had to get up and check on him again. How quiet the house could get before silence itself felt suspicious. Exhaustion stopped asking permission. It settled in and made itself useful. I had to find another way.

My only hope at rest was to limit the places he could go.

I turned his bedroom doorknob around. It wasn't a decision I announced or defended. It wasn't something I explained to anyone beforehand. It came from a racing heart, racing feet, and the knowledge that I could not always reach him in time. It came from counting the steps, the seconds, the space between us, and realizing I could lose him in that gap.

I slept right next door. The camera stayed on. The monitor never dimmed. I learned even finer details of sound—the handle turning, the shift of his weight against the door, the difference between movement and intention. I listened for everything. I was always listening.

Each adjustment after that stacked on the one before it. More cameras in the hallway. More safety locks on doors. Small changes that looked excessive from the outside and felt necessary from the inside. Every decision had the same purpose, even if I didn't say it out loud:

Protect him.

People had opinions. I stopped hearing them.

They weren't living it.

Their ears hadn't learned to catalog every sound in the house.

The creak of the floor just inside his bedroom door.

The particular weight of his footstep versus anyone else's.

The difference between a cabinet closing and a lock turning.

Their bodies didn't jolt awake at 2 a.m. to silence—because silence was never just silence anymore.

It was a question.

He had spent his career working in a prison. Caring for men whose freedom had been taken by the state. Watching patterns. Enforcing routines. Keeping people safe inside walls they didn't choose.

I had built this house to be open. Light. Air moving from room to room. A place where people gathered, where doors stayed unlocked, and laughter carried through.

Now I slept beside a monitor.

Now I counted steps and exits.

Now I turned a doorknob around and called it care.

It wasn't punishment.

It was the cost of protecting a person I loved with every fiber of me.

And I paid it willingly.

Chapter 27

The Unspeakable, Spoken Wish

The house never went dark anymore. It dimmed, as if it had also learned not to fully relax. Lamps stayed off. Screens stayed on. I lay on my side with one earbud in, phone angled just enough that I could see both the video and the feed at the same time, my body still and alert.

Darius popped his head into the doorway.

"He's all set. I'm going up," he said.

I pushed myself up on one elbow. "Does he have on a clean diaper? Did he give you any trouble?"

"Yeah, he's all cleaned up. In his bed. Just lying there." He paused, then added with that reflexive little chuckle, "Not sure he's gonna stay there."

I glanced at the monitor. Dad was in bed. The blanket rose and fell over him at a slow, even pace. No movement at the door. No shadow crossing the floor. It would've looked peaceful if I didn't know the rhythms of restlessness.

"Okay," I said. "Thanks."

Darius nodded and disappeared down the hall. I listened to his footsteps fade.

I could have been sleeping. Or that's what I told myself anyway.

Instead, I scrolled—an activity more aligned with the incessant patrol of my mind at night, always on.

Caregiver videos found me without effort now. I didn't search for them anymore. The algorithm learned faster than I ever could. Faces like mine filled the screen. Women my age, sitting on unmade beds or couches pushed up against walls, speaking calmly about lives that had narrowed around care. Their voices were steady, like they had already crossed whatever line I was approaching.

The woman on my screen sat on the edge of her bed, phone propped against a lamp. No makeup. Hair pulled back. She spoke for a long time before she got there, about love, about devotion, about doing everything right. About caring for her husband and losing him in inches instead of all at once. It was heartbreaking and validating at the same time, spoken the way people do when they've already made peace with saying it. Then she stopped.

Her eyes dropped out of frame for a second, like she was checking herself, like she was deciding whether to say what came next.

When she looked back up, her voice didn't shake.

She said that when it finally ended . . . she would feel relief.

The word hit me hard enough that I sat up, the mattress sinking beneath my hand.

Relief.

Not peace. Not closure. Not grief. Relief.

She didn't apologize for it. She didn't soften the word or dress it up. She didn't follow it with gratitude or guilt. She said it plainly, like a fact she had already made room for.

My chest tightened, not in protest but in recognition.

I looked back at the camera feed. Dad hadn't moved. The room looked exactly the same as it had a moment before, but something in me had shifted. I lowered the phone into my lap and stared at the dark edge of my room, the place where light stopped reaching.

The thought had already lived in me. I knew that. I just hadn't given it language.

Relief wouldn't mean I hadn't loved him. It wouldn't erase the years of care or the moments that still felt like him. It would mean the vigilance had stopped. The counting. The waiting. The constant readiness for something to go wrong.

It would mean no more listening for footsteps that shouldn't be there. No more bargaining with food. No more calculating how long I could leave a room before something happened.

It would mean the slow death I had already been living alongside him would finally end.

I held onto the edge of the mattress, grounding myself in the weight of my own body, the only thing in the room that still felt entirely mine.

Loving him and resenting the work required to keep him safe had been true at the same time for longer than I wanted to admit. Those two things had learned how to coexist inside me without canceling each other out.

I didn't say it out loud.

I didn't text anyone.

I didn't pray.

I let the word settle where it belonged.

That was what I wished for.

The quiet, unspeakable wish for relief.

The one you don't dare say out loud.

The one where, in the stillness of the night, you find yourself hoping that your loved one drifts off to sleep and is freed from their suffering.

Yes. I wished that my father would pass.

And when I let myself imagine it—when I truly let myself sit with what that moment would feel like—the only word that came to mind was relief.

I would be relieved.

Because the truth was that I had been watching him die a slow, painful, and arduous death for years. Day by day, piece by piece, I watched the man he was slip further and further away, and there was nothing I could do to stop it. It was gut-wrenching. It was exhausting. It was cruel. And it was complicated.

Because in the same breath that I felt gratitude for the laughter, the small moments of clarity, the brief glimpses of him, I also felt resentment when he fought me on the things I had to do to keep him safe. The diaper changes, the showering, the wandering—all these were cycles of patience and fury, love and frustration, deep connection and unbearable detachment.

Relief.

I said it to myself without flinching.

And for the first time, I didn't feel ashamed of it.

Chapter 28

The Slow Goodbyes

The house ran on routines the way a hospital runs on rounds. Not dramatic, not inspirational, just constant.

Mornings always started before my body was ready. The heat would kick on, the coffee would start, and Dad would already be sitting somewhere he wasn't supposed to be yet, waiting like the day owed him something. I learned not to speak too fast. Not to protect him, but to protect whatever patience I had left before breakfast.

Darius moved through it all like a man trying to solve a problem with his hands. He did laundry and carried laundry baskets. He took out the trash. He cleaned up the little messes before they turned into big ones. If Dad needed to be showered, he did it. If Dad needed to be changed, he did it. He never made a speech about it. He never announced he was tired. He just did the next thing.

And on paper, that looks like love.

In real life, it felt like living beside someone who thought a smile and a joke could keep things sane, and it only made me bitter.

I stood at the sink rinsing a plate that had barely been touched. Dad had pushed his food around for ten minutes like it was a puzzle, then looked at me with suspicion.

"What is that?" he asked.

"It's chicken," I said. "You like chicken."

He stared at it like I'd lied.

"I don't want that."

Darius was already up and opening the bread bag like he'd done it a hundred times.

"Here," he said, sliding a peanut butter and jelly sandwich in front of Dad.

Dad's eyes softened.

"That's better."

I didn't say anything. I just watched Dad take a bite and relax into it, as if all the pushback had never happened.

Darius stood at the counter afterward, wiping it down in long, efficient strokes.

"You okay?" he asked, not turning around.

It was a normal question, asked the way people ask when they want the answer to be "yeah."

I kept my hands under running water longer than I needed to, staring at the soap bubbles sliding down the drain.

"No," I said. "I'm not."

He nodded once.

"We'll figure it out."

I waited for something else. A second question. A pause that meant he was actually listening. Something that said, *Tell me. I'm here. I'm with you.*

Instead, he tossed the paper towel in the trash and glanced toward the hallway.

"You want me to take him up now?"

That was his language. Tasks. Order. Movement. Fixing.

And in the moment, I hated how grateful I still felt for it.

Later that night, I tried again. I wanted a deeper connection with him in our new roles, not just someone checking off the boxes with me.

Dad was finally in bed. I could hear Darius downstairs, the muted sounds of him locking up, checking doors, moving through the house the way you move through a place you don't fully trust anymore.

He came into my room and sat on the edge of the bed, waiting to see if I needed anything.

"Can I say something?" I asked.

"Sure."

I cringed. Not because I didn't know what to say, but because I knew what would happen when I said it.

"I feel like I'm losing my mind," I said. "I feel like I'm in this alone even when you're here."

His face shifted. His mouth pulled into that familiar half-smile that showed up when he didn't know what to do with what I was saying.

"You're not alone," he said quickly. "I'm here."

"I know you're HERE," I said. My voice rose before I could stop it. "I know you're physically here. That is not what I mean."

He looked at the camera monitor like it could rescue him.

"He's been rough lately," he said. "We just gotta keep doing what we're doing."

My hands clenched under the blanket. I could feel my pulse in my fingertips.

"I'm not talking about him," I said. "I'm talking about me."

Darius blinked, like he didn't understand the sentence.

"What do you want me to do?" he asked, and the frustration in his voice made it sound like I'd handed him a test he hadn't studied for.

"I want you to listen," I said. "I want you to ask me how I'm doing and then actually stay there when I answer. I want to be able to fall apart and not have you look at me like I'm creating a problem for you to solve."

He rubbed his hand over his face, slow and tired.

"I'm tired too, Tahnya."

"I know," I said, and it came out softer than I meant it to. "I know you are. I'm not competing with you. I'm telling you I'm drowning."

He exhaled hard, then stood up.

"I'm going to bed," he said.

Not angry. Not cruel. Just done. Like the conversation had a lid and he'd put it back on.

He walked out and left the door half-open, the way he always did, like he was keeping an eye on everything. Like he couldn't help himself.

I lay there staring at the camera feed. Dad was still. The blanket rose and fell. The house looked peaceful.

And I felt completely alone inside it, and angry.

The next day, Darius got up and did everything again. He made coffee. He checked the locks. He helped with Dad. He ran errands.

He didn't mention the night before.

That was his way. Keep moving. Don't make it worse. Don't stir it up.

So, I learned to speak less.

Not because I had nothing to say, but because I was tired of watching my words hit his face and slide off.

We started eating on the couch more often. Plates balanced on our knees, the TV volume up just enough to fill the space between us. Dad would wander in and out, sometimes sitting with us, sometimes standing in the doorway like he wasn't sure if he belonged there.

Darius would laugh at a commercial.

Dad would laugh too, just after him, as if he was laughing because he recognized laughter, not because he understood the joke.

I would look at the three of us in the reflection of the dark TV screen during a pause and think, *This is not what I pictured.*

At night, I retreated to my room. There, I didn't have to perform closeness I no longer felt. I didn't have to lie next to someone and pretend I wasn't alone. I could shut the door, turn off the lights, and let the night be exactly what it was.

We'd pass each other each day in the hall like coworkers changing shifts.

"How was he last night?"

"Restless. Up twice."

"Okay. I'll take first watch tonight."

Information exchanged. Nothing else required.

Weeks passed like that. Months, really. The house became a fine-tuned machine. Every system had a purpose. Every task had a place. Every person had a role.

Darius was the doer.

I was the orchestrator.

Brianna was the steady second set of hands, the one who showed up without hesitation, the one who could look at me and know what I needed before I said it.

Dad was the center of it all, unaware that every decision in the house now revolved around his needs.

I realized that my marriage had become logistics.

A schedule.

A rotation.

A quiet agreement to keep the thing running.

I didn't hate Darius. That's what made it worse.

If he had been cruel, if he had been careless, if he had been self-ish, it would've been easier to name. Easier to blame. Easier to leave.

But he was good.

He was trying.

He was doing what he knew how to do.

And still, I was disappearing inside the life we were managing.

Caregiving does that. It shrinks the room around you until there's barely space for anything else. Not romance. Not tenderness. Not softness. Not the messy conversations where someone has to hold your pain without fixing it.

Every night, when we all went to our respective corners, I felt the grief stack another layer over itself.

Not just grief for my father.

Grief for the marriage I was still standing inside but no longer felt held by.

Darius was there. Always there. Doing what needed to be done.

He just wasn't with me.

And somewhere in the middle of it all, I understood that I was losing two things at the same time.

My father.

And the version of my marriage I thought would carry me through this.

We didn't name it then.

We kept moving. Kept functioning. Kept showing up.

But I knew.

I knew because I had already started imagining my life on the other side of that house. Not a dramatic reinvention but a practical one. What I would sell. What I would keep. Where I would go when there was nothing left to manage but myself.

In my mind, the order was simple.

My father would pass.

I would sell the house.

I would leave.

I would be done.

Not because I didn't love my husband, but because I could no longer imagine a future that included rest inside our marriage. I stopped picturing us on the other side of my father's death, rebuilt and closer for having endured it together. That image no longer came when I tried to summon it.

I didn't say any of this out loud.

I carried it quietly, like a bruise you keep pressing just to make sure it's real.

I decided to keep going. To do the best I could with what I had. To let function be enough for now.

In those weeks, something permanently shifted.

I kept going, not because I believed we would find our way back, but because stopping would have broken everything at once.

Chapter 29

The Last Homecoming

It had been years.

Years of caregiving.

Not just the years of caring for my father through dementia, but all the years before that. The years—made up of hours, of days, of weeks—of caring for him when mental illness set in.

Years of watching my father disappear in inches while the rest of the world kept hurtling forward as if nothing was wrong.

Years of holding everything together while my own edges frayed.

Somewhere in that stretch of time, I became determined. Independent. Sharp.

People noticed, and their words mirrored their judgments, both the validating and the critical. "Confident," some called me. "Scrappy," "resilient," "resourceful, "bold," and, yes, "bossy."

That last word had followed me around since I was fourteen. Bossy. Too much. Too direct. Too controlling.

People always said it like it was a flaw.

They didn't see what built it. Didn't see why it was necessary to direct, to control.

Growing up, watching and learning about mental illness, I had no idea those early years were training me for this life.

It wasn't just my father.

It was my mother — the way she carried it, managed it, kept everything contained.

It was Ninette and her mother who didn't flinch. Didn't pull away. Always there when I needed somewhere to go.

The friend whose house I ran to that night, whose door was always open.

People who knew how to stand near it without making it worse.

All of them were teaching me, without any of us naming it, what it looked like to hold something you couldn't fix.

I didn't know they were shaping the woman I would need to become.

I didn't know mental illness and Alzheimer's would feel so close to each other.

The unpredictability.

The constant watch.

The way someone could still be standing in front of you and already be slipping.

Care. Compassion. Empathy. I learned these like learning the shape of my own body, not from theory or textbooks, but from standing beside someone who cannot save themselves and knowing your own system will fight for theirs.

I learned what it meant to be the person someone could rely on when their own body and mind stopped cooperating. I learned how to stay steady while everything else shook.

People close to me sometimes said I was too much.

Too assertive.

Too uncaring.

What they mistook for coldness was efficiency. What they called control was triage. What they labeled as emotional distance was the only way through.

Those traits got me through years of ups and downs. They allowed me to navigate uncertainty, make decisions no one wanted to make, and step into the role of caregiver when no one else could or would. I don't apologize for them. I don't soften them. I celebrate them.

Without them, I would not have survived.

And even with all that strength, all that preparation, nothing could have readied me for what came next in caring for my father in those final months.

I had been bracing myself for years, telling myself I was ready, rehearsing the ending in my head. And still, when it arrived, it hit like a tidal wave.

As 2023 closed and my father's decline became undeniable, everything I had built inside myself began to strain. Every carefully constructed wall. Every survival skill. Every ounce of toughness I relied on.

This wasn't just another downturn. I knew that.

It was the beginning of the end.

And no matter how many times I told myself I was prepared, I wasn't.

That Christmas, I didn't go all out.

I couldn't.

The energy simply wasn't there anymore. The nights had folded into days, the days into nights, until time lost its shape entirely. Exhaustion became the baseline. There was no reserve left to pull from.

We still gathered at my house.

We still laughed.

We still told stories.

Some moments felt warm. Almost normal.

But looking back, I see it now for what it was.

The last Christmas with Dad.

None of us knew it then.

By January, the signs were there, though we didn't understand what they were pointing to. He was having intestinal issues. Small things, at first. Things we explained away. Aging. Medication side effects. Dementia being dementia.

By February, we were trying harder. Doctor appointments.

Diet changes. More fiber. More water. The usual suggestions offered without urgency. Without answers.

Doctors didn't seem concerned.

So neither were we.

His faster decline became another thing to manage. Another adjustment to make. Another responsibility layered on top of everything else.

Everything came to a head almost four years to the day my caregiving journey began, before the sun was fully up.

"Mom!"

Brianna's voice cut through the house, sharp and panicked, pulling me out of sleep like a hand around my ankle.

"Mom. NOW."

I was running before my feet hit the floor. Down the hallway, my heart already racing, my body bracing itself the way it had learned to do over years of false alarms and real ones.

The smell hit first.

Sour. Metallic. Wrong.

Then I saw him.

He was bent forward on the bed, convulsing, vomiting with a force that didn't seem possible. His body shook with each heave, like it was coming from someplace deeper than his stomach. It was everywhere. The sheets. The floor. His clothes. His hands.

"I'm sorry," he kept saying between retches. "I'm sorry. I didn't mean to. I'm sorry."

He was shaking. Terrified. Trying to stop it with trembling hands, like he could contain what was happening if he just tried hard enough.

"It's okay, Dad," I said, already grabbing towels, already moving. "It's okay. You didn't do anything wrong."

But it wasn't stopping.

Nothing we did slowed it down.

"Breathe with me," Brianna tried to relax him, her voice tight as she held the bag under his chin. "Just breathe."

He tried. He really tried.

We didn't talk about what to do next. There was no discussion. No debate. We moved the way people do when they've been through countless emergencies.

Get him upright.

Get him a blanket.

Get shoes on.

My hands worked without instruction. Muscle memory. Years of practice.

Outside, the air was cold and gray. The car door slammed. My daughter climbed into the backseat with him, holding the bag, one hand braced against his chest.

"I'm right here, Gramps," she said. "I've got you."

He was still sick as we pulled out of the driveway.

The drive to the hospital felt suspended. Like time had folded in on itself. Every red light unbearable. Every mile compressed into something too tight to breathe inside.

"Almost there," I said as he groaned and leaned forward again. "We're almost there."

When we finally got into the ER, the lights inside were too bright. Too clean. Too indifferent.

We sat him in a wheelchair.

And then we waited.

Minutes turned into hours.

He slumped forward, exhausted, confused, still getting sick. Brianna sat on one side of him. I sat on the other. We watched the monitors. Watched the doors. Watched nurses walk past without looking at us.

"Mom," Brianna whispered at one point. "He looks really bad."

"I know," I said. "I know."

A nurse finally passed close enough that I stood up.

"Can you check his blood sugar?" I demanded.

She glanced at his chart. "Does he have diabetes?"

"Are you kidding me? YES, just check it," I said.

She hesitated, then nodded.

When she came back, her face had shifted just enough that my chest tightened before she even spoke.

"It's over 300," she said.

The number landed heavy.

Four years earlier.

The night we almost lost him.

Something old and sharp snapped into place inside me.

"No," I said. "That's not okay. You need to take him back. NOW."

She started to say something. Protocol. Wait times. Triage.

"I'm not asking," I said, my voice steady in a way that surprised even me. Every edge, every hard-earned instinct, every refusal to be dismissed, every bit of "bossy"—all of it came online. "He is not okay. You need to move. This has happened before. He needs to be back there now!"

And finally, *finally*, they took him back.

As they wheeled him down the hall, his eyes found mine.

"I don't feel well," he mumbled half awake, exhausted inside his reeling body.

"I know, Dad," I said, walking alongside the gurney. "We are getting you help. You're safe. I'm right here."

The days that followed blurred together in a way that made time unreliable. We moved from room to room, test to test, the hospital becoming a maze of waiting areas and hallways, and the ever-present smell of sanitizer and old sheets. I slept in pieces, if at all, always half-alert, listening for alarms or footsteps, waiting for someone to tell me what came next.

An MRI finally gave us something concrete. A large hernia. A blockage. Words that sounded clinical and manageable until I understood what they meant inside his body. Because my father had a DNR, there was no default path forward. Every decision, every next step, landed squarely on me. Not theoretically. Not eventually. Right then, in real time.

They came in with a tray and explained they needed to place a tube through his nose to drain the buildup in his stomach. The nurse spoke calmly, efficiently, as if this were routine. My father looked at her, then looked at me, confusion already spreading across his face.

"What are they doing?" he asked.

"They're going to help you feel better," I said, stepping closer to the bed, even as my chest tightened.

The first attempt was rough. He gagged immediately, his hands flying up instinctively as his body reacted before his mind could catch up. They pulled the tube out and said they'd try again. The second attempt was worse. He began retching violently, his body jerking against the bed, his eyes wide with fear.

"I don't like this," he said, his voice strained. "Please."

By the third attempt, panic had fully set in. He didn't understand where he was or why people were holding him down. He kept turning his head toward me, searching my face, asking me to make it stop. Each time they withdrew the tube, he continued retching, his body trapped in a reflex it could not shut off.

"This isn't working," I said, my voice sharp now. "He doesn't understand what's happening."

"We need to get it placed," someone replied, already preparing for the next try.

The fourth and fifth attempts felt unbearable to witness. His resistance weakened, not because he agreed, but because he was exhausted. His voice grew hoarse. His hands trembled.

Each attempt stripped something from him, dignity bleeding away under the guise of procedure.

Then suddenly, the room changed.

Black bile poured from him, thick and dark, coming with a force that stunned everyone into stillness. It kept coming, spilling onto the bed, onto the floor, onto him. One nurse swore quietly. Another nurse froze mid-motion. I stood there, unable to move, watching something leave his body that felt final.

This was no longer treatment. This was his body refusing.

A doctor I hadn't seen before stepped in and waved everyone back. He lowered his voice and sat down in front of me, eye level. He didn't rush. He didn't speak in jargon. He spoke to me like a person.

"I'm sorry," he said. "This shouldn't have gone on like that."

He explained that the only remaining option for my father was an endoscopy. But they would have to put him under anesthesia. Doing anything while he was awake was no longer possible. He described the hernia, how my father's stomach had shifted into his chest cavity, and the hope was to drain it and relieve the pressure.

Then he paused.

"If this doesn't work," he said carefully, "the next step would be major surgery."

He looked at me, really looked, and his expression softened.

"If it were my father," he said, "I wouldn't put him through it."

The room seemed to narrow around us. Another decision settled heavily into my hands. I knew exactly what those words meant, and I knew exactly what my father had wanted long before we ever reached this point.

After that conversation, time warped into unrecognizable shapes. The days stretched and collapsed at the same time, long and hollow, marked only by medication schedules and the beep of hospital machines. Nadene and I took turns in the room, never fully leaving, never fully resting. Someone always had to be awake. If we both slept, even briefly, he would reach for the tube.

We made a system without discussing it. One of us stayed in the chair, upright, eyes trained on his hands. The other curled onto the narrow couch, sleeping in shallow bursts, shoes still on, phone clenched like an alarm. Between the two of us, we might have gotten three hours of sleep a night. Sometimes less. The room never fully darkened. Monitors glowed. Hallway lights spilled under the door. Nurses moved in and out quietly, their voices low, their footsteps careful.

When he woke, his hands moved before his eyes opened. Muscle memory, the instinct to relieve discomfort. He tugged at the unfamiliar weight taped to his face, confused and irritated by something he could not understand.

"No, Dad," one of us would say quickly, reaching for his wrist. "It has to stay."

Sometimes he looked at us with suspicion, as if we were part of whatever was being done to him. Other times, his face softened with relief, like he was grateful someone was there. He begged us to take the NG tube out of his nose. Then, just as often, he tried to do it himself, fingers clumsy but determined.

They put mittens on his hands to stop him from pulling at what to him was just an uncomfortable foreign object that he didn't understand and was there without his consent. Soft restraints, they called them. We hated the word, but we understood the need. The mittens were white and bulky, absurd against the seriousness of the moment.

So, we drew faces on them with big eyes, lopsided smiles, anything to make them look less like restraints. We turned his hands into puppets, talked to him through them, waved them gently in front of his face, hoping distraction might buy us a few minutes of calm.

Sometimes it worked. He would watch them, amused or curious, his breathing slowing as he focused on the movement. Sometimes he laughed. Other times, he stared straight through them, already drifting somewhere we couldn't follow.

When we played music for him, he settled more easily. Old songs. Familiar melodies. The kind that lived deeper than memory. His face would relax. His eyes close. For a few minutes at a time, his body rested.

Then the hallucinations returned.

He spoke to people who weren't there. Fought battles we couldn't see. His hands clenched and released as if gripping something just out of reach. We answered him anyway, grounding him as best we could, even when we didn't know what he was seeing.

He slipped out of the mittens. Once. Then again. Fast Eddie. Mr. Houdini. Even then, disease overtaking him, some stubborn, familiar part of him refused to be contained. It broke my heart and made me smile at the same time.

Five days passed like that. Five days of watching, waiting, intervening. Five days of knowing, deep in my soul, that this was not turning around.

In that timeless, endless stretch, I often thought about what my father had said long before any of this:

"No heroics. Just let me go."

The clarity of it stayed with me, even as everything else unraveled.

During the day, Bri came with my mother, giving Nadene and me a chance to trade off and eat something that resembled food in the cafeteria. My mother sat close to the bed, holding his hand, speaking to him softly, even when he didn't respond. Brianna hovered at the foot of the bed, watching his face, learning his breathing, asking questions she already knew the answers to. We traded updates in hushed voices in the hallway, piecing together rest schedules and medication times like a relay race.

When the doctors came back in and spoke about the next steps, there was no argument left in me. No bargaining. No illusion that more time or intervention would give us anything but more suffering.

The decision, when it finally came, felt both devastating and inevitable.

He would come home on hospice.

And we all understood what that meant.

This would be his last homecoming.

Chapter 30

The Final Goodbye

The house had a different sound now. There was no shuffle of his footsteps in the night. No sound of a man trying to find his way home. In its place was the uneven rhythm of his breathing down the hall.

I sat beside his bed, watching the slow, rhythmic rise and fall of his chest, knowing that, soon, it wouldn't rise again. I had been preparing for this moment for weeks, years even. But how do you truly prepare for that final goodbye?

Visitors had come and gone. Some whispered their farewells, pressing his hands between theirs, their words thick with love and sorrow. Others sat in silence, simply existing in the space with him, as if their presence alone could carry him peacefully across the threshold. Every day from March 11 to April 2, 2024, stretched on like a lifetime. The waiting was unbearable. I just wanted him to slip away gently, to find peace. I whispered to him often, hoping he could hear me, hoping my voice would somehow remind him that it was okay to let go.

The day before he came home from the hospital, I made sure his room was ready for a peaceful passing. If this was how his story was going to end, then I would make damn sure it ended with dignity, in comfort, surrounded by love.

Darius and Diego ripped up the carpet, stripping away the stains, the remnants of illness that had seeped into the fibers. I refused to let my father's last days be spent in a space that smelled of sickness, with memories of struggle woven into the space around him. We laid down a new floor—temporary, but clean, fresh—a reset. I set up a TV, positioned chairs for those who wanted to sit with him, and lit soft, flickering candles that cast a warm glow across the room. I played relaxing music. Music that made you exhale a little deeper; music that could carry someone gently into the next world.

My sister and niece were there often. My mother, almost daily. The hospice nurses moved through the house with a gentleness I will never forget. Friends came by. Neighbors who had known him for years. One by one, they said their goodbyes. And for a while, he still responded. A small smile, a flicker of recognition.

But as the days went on, his body followed the path I was told it would. He began seeing things in the corners of the room. At first, he would point, wordless, and smile. I liked to think he was seeing his mother, brothers, and sisters. Friends long gone, waiting for him. Then came the death rattle. His breathing became labored, like the weight of life was pressing down on him one last time, with the need for constant medication. Keeping him comfortable became the only thing that mattered. I didn't want him to feel an ounce of pain. He had carried enough of that in his lifetime.

And yet, I still had a schedule. Even as his life faded, the structure I created as a caregiver didn't stop. Brianna, my savior in this process, took the night shifts. I took the days. And we were so tired. Caregiving had already drained me, but this? This was a whole new level of exhaustion. A soul-deep kind of fatigue settled into my bones. My body finally gave in. I felt sick, worn down, but I pushed through. Because I knew that, soon, he wouldn't be here.

And then, the night came.

I had sent Bri home to rest. It was just me, my husband, and my father. The room was still—waiting. I turned to Darius. "Go to bed," I told him. "If I need anything, I'll wake you." He nodded and disappeared down the hall, leaving just us.

I sat beside my father, listening to his uneven breathing—sometimes steady, sometimes pausing just long enough to make my heart stop. I felt myself fading, my body begging for sleep. So, at 1:30 AM, I leaned over, took his hand in mine, and whispered into his ear. "Dad, I'm tired. I know you know how much you were loved. How much I love you. I'm going to go take a nap, and it's okay if you're not here when I come back. It's time to let go and go to sleep." I covered him with his blanket, propped his pillow gently beneath his head, and kissed his forehead one last time.

Then, I walked to my room. I laid down, expecting to sleep for hours. But just thirty minutes later, I shot awake. There was no sound. No rattle. No breath. Just silence.

I already knew.

I walked back to his room, my heart pounding, but not with panic, with knowing.

And there he was at peace.

I placed my hand on his cheek, just like I had the night this all began, when I found him unconscious in his chair, still alive but barely. But this time, he was cold. He was gone.

I stood there, letting it hit me. The grief. The weight. The emptiness. I would never see his smile again. I would never hear his voice. I would never again have to watch him struggle against the betrayals of his own mind. And then, I felt what that woman on the video foretold.

Relief.

It arrived quietly, without ceremony. No rush. No wave. Just a loosening, deep in my chest, like something that had been clenched for years, finally let go.

I waited for guilt to follow it.

For shame.

For the internal scolding that said this was wrong, that a good daughter shouldn't feel anything but devastation.

But it didn't come.

What came instead was a breath and the understanding that his suffering had ended. That the long, slow unraveling of his mind and body was finally over. That the man who had been trapped inside himself for so long was free from the confusion, the fear, and the constant fight against a world he no longer recognized.

I stood there, my hand still resting on his cheek, tracing the familiar shape of his face. His features were softer now. Unburdened. The tension that had lived in his jaw, in his brow, in the set of his mouth, was gone.

He looked like himself again.

I thought about the man he had been before all of this. The sound of his laugh. The way he sat in a room like he had nowhere else to be. The stories he told. The way he filled a room without trying. The way he loved would stay with me.

That man had been slipping away for years, piece by piece, memory by memory. I had been saying goodbye long before this night.

Loving someone through a death like that changes you. It stretches grief across years instead of moments. It asks you to mourn while the person is still breathing. It teaches you that relief and love are not opposites. They are companions.

This moment was not the beginning of my grief.

It was the end of my watch.

I had lived on high alert for so long that I didn't immediately know what to do with the stillness. There would be no more listening for footsteps. No more calculating medication times. No more bracing for the next crisis. No more asking my body to stay awake just a little longer.

The house felt different now. Not empty. Finished.

I sat there longer than I needed to, letting the reality settle into my bones. Letting myself feel the ache of loss alongside the undeniable peace of knowing I would never have to watch him suffer again.

Eventually, I stepped back and covered him more fully with the blanket, smoothing it the way I had done a thousand times before. Muscle memory. Habit. Care. Only this time, there was no next task waiting. I left the room quietly and called up the stairs for Darius.

He came down, half asleep, wiping his eyes.

"He's gone."

"I'm sorry," he said, pulling me close.

I called my mother and sister, Bri, hospice, and the funeral home. They all arrived in the early hours of that morning. The hospice nurse offered her condolences and walked us through next steps. How to destroy the medications that kept him comfortable, and what services they offered for grieving families.

The funeral director arrived with his father, both in full suits, telling us there was no rush. I informed them we had already said our goodbyes. Then I hung a curtain between the living room and the front door so my mother and Bri wouldn't have to see them carry him out.

Once it was all done, I walked up to my room and, for the first time in years, I slept.

And just like that, with the light of the next day, the grief was there. Of course it was. It would always be there, in some form.

But so was something else.

A stillness.

A release.

A deep, unshakable knowing that I had done right by him.

His life had ended with dignity.

His suffering with mercy.

And my long vigil had ended with love.

He was free.

And for the first time in years, so was I.

Chapter 31

The Funeral

I opened my eyes to gray morning light filtering through the blinds and immediately felt it—the itch. That maddening, relentless throb that had been building for days. A deep, crawling burn that lived inside, and no amount of shifting or adjusting made any difference.

Stress had manifested into a yeast infection and Monistat couldn't touch it. My body felt like it was falling apart from the inside out, every cell screaming that I'd been running on empty for too long.

I threw the covers back and sat up, my skin prickling with discomfort. Every position was wrong. Sitting hurt. Standing would hurt. Walking would be unbearable. But lying there wasn't an option either.

The funeral was today.

I pressed my palms against my eyes and took one long breath, trying to will my body into cooperation. It didn't work. The itch pulsed, insistent and cruel, a physical manifestation of four years of exhaustion I could no longer ignore. But, as always, I still had to keep going.

When I opened the bedroom door, sound rushed in like a wave.

I heard footsteps overhead. Drawers opening and closing. Voices pitched low in that hushed funeral-morning register, quiet enough to seem respectful, loud enough to ensure I'd hear them. My house had been invaded by helpers. Well-meaning relatives unpacking bags in guest rooms. Friends rearranging my kitchen like they lived here. Everyone moving with that performative usefulness that always follows death.

I just need to get through today.

The thought arrived fully formed, a mantra I'd repeat a hundred times before noon.

I moved down the hallway, every step a small act of rebellion against my body's protest. The bathroom mirror showed me a woman who looked like she'd aged a decade in a week. Dark circles beneath her eyes. Skin drained of color. Hair flattened on one side from restless sleep.

I splashed water on my face, but it didn't help. Nothing would.

In the kitchen, the assault began before I'd taken three steps.

The smell hit first. Coffee, thank God. But underneath it, the cloying sweetness of baked goods, the butter-heavy scent of croissants, and that thick, funeral-flower scent that had somehow migrated from the living room. Lilies. I'd always loved lilies. But today, the smell was too much, too insistent, the olfactory equivalent of someone grabbing your face and saying, *Look at me. Feel something.*

I moved toward the coffee maker out of habit, dodging my sister who was pulling plates from the cabinet.

"Morning," she said, her voice careful. "How'd you sleep?"

"I didn't."

She nodded like she'd expected that answer and went back to arranging the barrage of items on the kitchen island.

The counter was buried. Foil pans still warm from someone's oven. Store-bought muffins in plastic clam shells that nobody would eat. A basket of bagels with six different cream cheese options spread around it like satellites. Flowers crammed into every available vase, and several that weren't in vases at all. A mixing bowl. A pitcher. A goddamn mason jar.

My kitchen had turned into a grief buffet.

My phone vibrated against the counter. I glanced at the screen. Seventeen missed calls. Thirty-two text messages. All of them variations on the same theme:

So sorry for your loss. Thinking of you today. He's in a better place. Let me know if you need anything.

I turned the phone face down and poured coffee into the largest mug I could find.

Behind me, my mother's voice drifted in from the living room. "What time are we leaving? When is everyone getting here?"

"I think Tahnya said 12:30," my sister called back without looking up.

"12:30! Isn't that too early?"

"It's so we have time alone before people start showing up."

I closed my eyes and took a long sip of coffee, letting the heat move through me. Outside the window, the world was continuing as if nothing had changed. A neighbor walking their dog. Dew glistening on the grass. A car starting up across the street, engine coughing in the cold.

Inside, people kept moving through my kitchen, opening cabinets they'd never opened before, looking for serving spoons and napkins and plates they'd never use again after today. Each person acting out their idea of usefulness because sitting still with grief felt impossible.

My niece appeared in the doorway, already dressed in black, makeup carefully applied.

"You okay, Aunt Tahnna?"

"Yeah, I'm fine. I'll be okay."

She looked at me like she didn't believe me but knew better than to push. "You need help with anything?"

"No. Thank you."

She hovered for another minute or two, then drifted back toward the living room.

I stood there gripping my mug, the discomfort flaring again, a reminder that my body was actively betraying me on the day I most needed it to cooperate. It was done holding back the bone-deep exhaustion from years of holding everything together, and now that the scaffolding was gone, the whole structure was collapsing.

Just get through today.

I set the mug down and headed back upstairs before anyone

could ask me another question I didn't have the energy to answer.

I stood in front of the closet and stared at the clothes I'd laid out the night before.

The black dress.

I'd chosen it carefully, knee-length, fitted but not tight, elegant enough for a funeral without trying too hard. But looking at it now, I knew immediately it was wrong. The thought of wearing hose underneath that dress felt like one more unnecessary cruelty. As if the day hadn't already demanded enough, as if my body hadn't already paid its dues. Too clingy. And I knew my body wouldn't cooperate. I couldn't sit through a funeral in that. Couldn't stand in a receiving line, couldn't greet mourners, couldn't make small talk with distant relatives while every nerve screamed in protest.

I shoved the dress aside and pulled out black pants. Loose. Breathable. A cream blouse that wouldn't cling. Flat shoes that wouldn't punish my swollen feet.

No bold jewelry. Just my wedding ring and small gold studs.

I dressed slowly, every movement deliberate, trying to minimize friction against oversensitive skin. When I finally got the pants buttoned, I stood in front of the mirror and barely recognized myself.

A woman dressed to show up. Not to shine. Not to impress. Just to get through the day.

I ran the flat iron through my pixie cut, smoothing out the curls I usually wore. The heat felt good against my scalp, one small point of control in a morning that felt entirely out of my hands.

My reflection stared back, hair straight, clothes plain, eyes ringed with shadows that my concealer couldn't hide.

This was the familiar version of me that people would remember from today. Steady. Composed. The woman who held it together.

They wouldn't see the sleepless nights. The way my hands shook slightly as I set the flat iron down. They wouldn't know that I'd been awake at 2 AM googling how long grief was supposed to last, or that I'd cried in the shower yesterday for the first time since he died.

They'd see what I let them see.

And that would have to be enough.

As we pulled into the parking lot, my hands stayed on the steering wheel longer than necessary. The building sat there waiting, brick and neutral and indifferent, like it had done this a thousand times before and would do it a thousand times after us. I watched a flag stir slightly at the edge of the lot, the fabric lifting and falling without urgency, and thought, *So this is where he ends.*

I didn't want to get out of the car yet. Once my feet hit the pavement, the day would officially start. Once the door opened, there would be no more pretending this was still private, still ours. I took a breath and felt it catch halfway down, my chest tight, my jaw already clenched.

The funeral director met us at the door, voice low, movements practiced and gentle. He nodded once, then stepped aside and ushered us in. "Take your time," he said. "It's just family for now."

Just inside the entrance, the memories started immediately. Poster boards lined the wall, photos taped carefully along the edges. Sixty-plus years flattened into foam core and glossy paper. Black-and-white shots from before I existed. Wedding photos. Babies balanced on their hips. Holidays. Vacations. A lifetime arranged in rows, smiling back at strangers. No one sat yet. We hovered, none of us ready to take a seat for something this final.

The room was arranged like a theater. Rows of chairs facing forward, waiting. The lights were low but not dim; all of it meant to feel respectful, not dramatic. The urn sat on a long table at the front of the room, almost hidden beneath flowers. Dozens and dozens of them. Blues and whites, soft greens, peace lilies arching outward like they were trying to create space around it. Roses. Hydrangeas. Arrangements sent with notes I hadn't read yet, and I wasn't sure I ever would. Love translated into petals and ribbon.

The clock was placed on a small table at the front of the room, surrounded, as if the flowers were bracing it, protecting it, or maybe just trying to distract from how small it was.

Behind it, in the back corner of the room, a video played on a loop. A steady stream of images dissolving into one another. My father laughing at a picnic table. Standing on a beach. Holding babies. Sitting at a kitchen table mid-story, mouth open, hands in motion. The motion never stopped. Even when no one was watching, his life kept moving forward frame by frame.

"It's beautiful," I said to the director. "Thank you."

I stepped closer to the table and stopped.

The clock was beautiful. Walnut casing, deep brown, polished to a soft sheen. The face was clean and white, the numbers silver, catching the light when I moved. Elegant. Heavy. Intentionally chosen.

My father had always loved watches. The weight of them. The mechanics. The idea that something small and precise could measure something as vast as a life. He liked knowing what time it was. Liked being on time. Liked the order of it. The predictability.

When I chose the clock, it felt right. Not sentimental. Honest.

Time had been the thing that took him. Slowly. Patiently. Without asking permission. Time stretched. Time dragged. Time repeated itself in endless loops of care and confusion and waiting. And then, at the end, time did something cruel and efficient. It stopped asking anything of him at all.

Now it sat there, holding what was left of him inside it, marking minutes he would never experience again.

The irony wasn't lost on me. A man who loved time, sealed inside an object designed to track it. A life reduced to something that ticks on without him.

I stared at it longer than I meant to.

That's all that's left, I thought.

Not the sound of his voice. Not the way he filled a room. Not the weight of his presence sitting next to you on a couch. Just this. Wood. Metal. Ash.

Time, arranged neatly on a table, surrounded by flowers trying their best to soften the truth.

I turned away before the thought could sink any deeper.

My sister appeared at my elbow. "You okay?"

"I'm fine."

"You don't look fine."

"I really am," I said again, sharper this time.

She studied my face for another moment, then let it go.

Movement at the door pulled my attention.

Collin stood in the doorway.

He was dressed in a dark suit, Angel just behind him. But it was his face that stopped me cold. He looked lost. Young in a way I hadn't seen in years. His eyes scanned the room like he was trying to orient himself, and when they finally landed on me, everything collapsed.

Not gradually.

All at once.

Like a building going down.

He crossed the room in five long strides, not running but moving with purpose, and the second he reached me, his knees buckled. I caught him. All six feet five inches, one hundred and ninety pounds of him folded into my arms, his weight pressing down, his breath coming in ragged, uneven gasps against my shoulder.

"Mom—"

The word cracked open, splintering into something raw and unfinished. Nothing else would come. Just that single syllable, choked and desperate.

Angel stood a few feet back, her own eyes filling with tears, giving us space. Around us, conversations stopped. My mother's hand flew to her mouth. My sister turned, startled. But I didn't look at any of them.

I just held him.

One hand on the back of his head, cradling it the way I used to when he was small. The other arm wrapped across his shoulders, anchoring him, holding him upright when his body wanted to collapse entirely.

"I know, Bubba," I whispered against his temple. "I know."

His whole body shook with crying that doesn't make a sound at first. Just steals all the air and leaves you gasping.

I felt the wet heat of his tears soaking through my blouse. Felt his fingers grip the fabric at my back like he was trying to hold on to something solid in a world that had suddenly shifted beneath him.

"I can't—" he managed, voice breaking apart. "I just—I can't believe he's—"

"You don't have to say anything," I told him, my own throat closing around the words. "You don't have to say anything at all."

We stood there, swaying slightly, while the room held its breath around us.

This was my son.

The boy who used to sit on the deck with his grandfather, talking about shoes and respect and slang that made no sense to either of them. The young man who was about to get married, who would walk down an aisle in a year without his grandfather there to see it. Who had spent countless afternoons watching westerns and eating peanut butter and jelly sandwiches while his gramps told him the same stories on repeat, never once showing impatience.

When he finally pulled back, his face was red and swollen, eyes searching mine like I might have an answer to a question he couldn't articulate.

"He loved you so much," I said quietly, my hands still on his shoulders. "You know that, right? He was so proud of you."

Collin nodded, wiping his face with the back of his hand, trying to pull himself together. His jaw worked like he was chewing on words he couldn't quite spit out.

"Yeah," he whispered finally. "Yeah, I know."

He straightened, shoulders pulling back, and I watched him rebuild himself in real time. The composure sliding back into place like armor. Angel stepped forward, slipping her hand into his, and he squeezed it hard.

"You good?" I asked.

He nodded again, not trusting his voice yet.

"Go sit," I said gently. "I'll be right there."

He moved toward the chairs with Angel, and I stood there another moment, letting the weight of it settle.

My sister touched my arm. "That was hard to watch."

I nodded, not trusting myself to speak.

Bri appeared, her face already streaked with tears. She didn't say anything, just wrapped her arms around me and held on. I hugged her back, feeling her shoulders shake.

"I miss him," she whispered.

"I know, Bri. Me too."

We stayed like that for a long moment, the family clustered together in the quiet funeral home before the space filled with strangers and condolences and all the performance grief requires.

The funeral director appeared in the doorway, checking his watch discreetly.

"We'll open the doors in about ten minutes," he said softly. "Just let me know if you need more time."

I nodded my thanks.

Ten more minutes of this stillness. This intimacy. Just us and him and the impossible smallness of that clock-shaped urn.

Then the doors would open, and I'd have to be the version of myself everyone expected.

But for now, I could just be his daughter.

Chapter 32

Eclipse

At first, I thought it was just the usual murmur of people settling in, voices low and respectful. But then the funeral director approached me, his expression slightly apologetic.

"Excuse me," he said softly. "I don't mean to interrupt, but the eclipse—it's starting now. If anyone would like to step out and see it, this would be the time."

My mother looked uncertain, but my sister was already standing. "Come on, Ma. Let's go see."

We filed out slowly, the immediate family first, then gradually others who'd been waiting in the lobby. The parking lot filled with people tilting their faces skyward, some holding those flimsy eclipse glasses, others just squinting against the weird half-light.

The sun was disappearing.

Slowly, methodically, a dark shadow crept across its face like something being erased. The temperature dropped. The shadows on the pavement stretched long and sharp, wrong for midday. Birds went quiet.

Around me, people gasped. Murmured. A few laughed nervously, that uncomfortable sound people make when they're witnessing something they don't understand.

I stood still, hands clasped in front of me, and watched.

The moon slid fully in front of the sun, and for a few seconds, the world went still. Twilight at noon. Stars appearing in a sky that shouldn't hold them yet.

"It's beautiful," someone whispered.

"Unbelievable," another agreed.

Then, as quickly as it had disappeared, the light began to return. The shadow receding. The sun reemerging, bright and insistent, as if nothing had happened at all.

When the eclipse passed, people began drifting back inside, still buzzing with the strangeness of it. But Brianna stayed beside me, her face tilted toward the sky even as the light normalized.

"Mom," she said softly.

I turned.

Her eyes were welling with tears, but she was smiling. Holding too many emotions at once.

"It's like heaven knew," she whispered. "Like it was ready for Gramps."

I looked at her, this young woman who had held my father's hand through the worst of it. Who had changed his diapers and crushed his pills and redirected him when he got confused.

"You gave him dignity," I said. "When this bullshit disease tried to take everything from him, you gave him dignity. And love. And laughter. He may have thought you were security, or those guys, and he may not have remembered your name every day, but he felt safe with you. I know he did."

Bri nodded, wiping her face again, trying to pull herself together.

"I'm not ready to go back in yet," she said quietly.

"Then we won't," I said.

We stood there a few minutes longer, the parking lot emptying around us, the sun fully restored now, bright and indifferent.

The eclipse wasn't reverence for me. It wasn't cosmic acknowledgment or divine timing or any of the things people were already whispering about.

It was just a reminder.

A body blocking the sun. A temporary darkening. A return to light.

Just like the last four years.

A long shadow, now lifting.

But for Bri, it was something else.

A moment to let herself break. To admit that her grandfather, the man she'd cared for, laughed with, protected, and loved was really gone. That the grief she'd been holding at bay during his slow decline had finally arrived in full force.

And she didn't have to hold it together anymore.

Not for him. Not for me. Not for anyone.

"I'm gonna miss him every single day," she said finally, her voice barely above a whisper.

"Me too," I said.

She looked at me then, really looked at me, and I saw it, the same exhaustion I carried. The same relief mixed with sorrow. The same gratitude for what we'd been able to give him, and the same grief for what we'd lost along the way.

"We did good, didn't we?" she asked.

"Yeah," I said, my own tears finally spilling over. "We did really good."

She nodded, took one last deep breath, and straightened her shoulders.

"Okay," she said. "I'm ready now."

We walked back inside together, side by side, and rejoined the others.

People had begun arriving in earnest now.

The funeral director opened the main doors, and the crowd filtered in slowly. Friends. Neighbors. Coworkers. Distant relatives, I hadn't seen in years. They moved through the space with that solemnity people reserve for funerals, their voices hushed and their movements careful.

The receiving line formed without anyone directing it. Muscle memory from a lifetime of attending these things. My mother at one end, with my aunt and my father's brother, one of the last standing from a family of thirteen. Me in the middle with

Darius. Collin and Brianna with their fiancés. My sister and her fiancé, my niece beside them. A small assembly line of condolences.

They filed past slowly, one by one, each person gripping my hand just a little too long, their faces arranged in practiced sympathy.

"He's in a better place."

I nodded.

"You did everything you could."

I smiled.

"He's not suffering anymore."

"Thank you."

"Such a good man. Always so kind."

"Yes. He was."

My face performed the script while my mind drifted somewhere above the scene, watching from a distance. I counted ceiling tiles. Twenty-four across. Noticed a water stain in the corner. Wondered if anyone else saw it or if grief made you notice things that didn't matter.

A cousin I hadn't seen in years squeezed my hand. "How are you holding up?"

"I'm okay."

"If you need anything—"

"I know. Thank you."

He moved down the line, and someone else took his place. An old friend. A neighbor from my mother's building—one of the nuns. Then another. Four or five of them moved through, some with canes, all offering prayers and assurances they'd look after her. Someone's husband whose name I'd forgotten, came down the line. And, of course, my tribe. The parade continued, each person offering the same words in slightly different arrangements, like they were working from a template.

A neighbor from the old block, whose house backed up to ours, reached for my hand.

"Your father was such a wonderful man," he said, tears in his eyes.

I squeezed his hand back and nodded, grateful he'd come.

The line continued until finally, mercifully, it ended.

The funeral director stepped to the front of the room. "Please, everyone, take your seats. We'll begin in just a moment."

The room settled, chairs shuffling, voices dropping to whispers. I sat in the front row between my mother and Darius, hands folded in my lap, and waited.

Our pastor stood to speak. She didn't need notes. She'd known my father for years, watched him laugh at backyard barbecues, heard his stories, seen him dance. When she talked about Fast Eddie, she didn't use platitudes or broad strokes. She used specifics.

His kindness. His humor. The way he'd greet you like you mattered, even on his worst days. The respect he carried, even when the disease tried to strip it away.

Her voice was steady and warm. She spoke like someone who had sat beside him, who knew the shape of his life beyond the obituary.

When she finished, the room sat in the kind of silence that only comes after truth has been spoken out loud.

I reached over and squeezed my aunt's hand. She was crying quietly, nodding.

"That was beautiful," I whispered.

She nodded again, unable to speak.

When the pastor finished, Bri stood, flanked by my son and my niece. They moved to the front together, shoulders touching, a folded piece of paper clutched in her hand.

She cleared her throat, voice already shaking.

"This is a letter," she began, "from one of our grandmother's best friends. She couldn't be here today, but she wanted us to read this for her."

The three of them passed the page between them, each taking a few lines, their young voices wavering but steady.

The letter was warm. Full of small memories. My father's laugh, his kindness, the way he'd always ask how you were doing and wait for the answer. Gratitude for a friendship that had spanned decades. Admiration for a man who had lived with grace despite hardship.

I watched them, my kids and my niece, standing up there holding each other's weight, and something in my chest cracked open.

They weren't just reading words.

They were carrying a legacy forward.

When they finished, the room was silent. They returned to their seats, and I reached for my daughter's hand as she sat down beside me.

"You did good," I whispered.

She nodded, unable to speak, tears streaming freely now.

The funeral director stepped forward quietly, his hands clasped. "Thank you all for being here today. The family invites you to join them at The Century House for a meal and continued celebration of Eddie's life. The address is on the card you received." He paused, then added softly, "Please take your time."

People began standing, gathering their coats and purses, drifting toward the doors in small clusters. The formality dissolved into something looser. People began hugging. Whispering. Making plans to meet at the restaurant.

I stayed seated, letting the room empty around me.

My eyes drifted back to the clock urn at the front of the room, still surrounded by flowers. I stood to glance at the video loop still playing in the background, the images dissolving into one another, endlessly repeating, like he was stuck in a moment that would never move forward.

I thought about all the times I'd watched him forget. Watched him search for words that wouldn't come. Watched him look at me with confusion, trying to place my face in a memory that kept slipping away.

But sitting there, watching those images cycle through, I realized something.

He wasn't stuck anymore.

The loop had finally stopped.

Darius touched my shoulder gently. "You ready?"

I took one last look at the clock, at the flowers, at the empty chairs that had held a room full of people who loved him.

"Yeah," I said quietly. "Let's go."

Chapter 33

Full Circle

The restaurant was full by the time we arrived.

We hadn't picked just any restaurant—this was the place where, more than fifty years earlier, my mother had brought my father to meet her parents for the first time. This was the place where their story began. And now, in a way, it held its closing chapter.

They'd set up round tables draped in white tablecloths and wrapped the silverware in cloth napkins. Someone had clearly spent time on the centerpieces too—flowers and small votives arranged just so.

My mother sat with her brother and sister, the three of them clustered together in quiet companionship. From across the room, I watched her lean toward them, hands folded neatly on the table, nodding as they spoke in low voices. She looked smaller somehow. Older. Aging that happens overnight when you lose the person who's been beside you for half a century.

I couldn't stay in one place.

I moved from table to table, checking in on cousins I hadn't seen in years, hugging old friends, making small talk with people whose names I'd forgotten but whose faces carried decades of shared history. My smile stayed in place. My voice never cracked. I played host while my body ran on muscle memory.

The room buzzed with conversation. Forks scraped against plates. Glasses clinked. Somewhere, one of our old neighbors was laughing, I assume telling a story about my father, the sound rising above everything else. It looked, for all the world, like a celebration.

Except the clock-shaped urn wasn't there, but its presence, like time, cast a shadow over everything.

At one point, my mother glanced around the restaurant, her eyes sweeping over the familiar tables and chairs, the same layout she'd seen decades ago when everything was ahead of them instead of behind.

"This is where it all began," she said quietly, more to herself than anyone else.

But I heard.

I paused mid-conversation with a cousin and turned toward her. Our eyes met across the room. She gave a small, sad smile.

Beginning and end. Full circle.

The weight of it settled over me like a blanket I couldn't shake off.

I stayed another hour, maybe longer, moving through the room, nodding at the right moments, laughing when it seemed appropriate, accepting condolences I had already heard a hundred times that day. Each one landed softer than the last, repetition dulling even the sharpest things. Eventually, the crowd thinned, servers started clearing plates with practiced efficiency, and the restaurant slowly returned to itself.

When it was finally over, I thanked the staff and the owner. Their faces held a careful kindness, the kind reserved for endings that don't belong to you but still ask something of you. I gathered my coat, my purse, and the framed photograph of my father that had been displayed near the entrance. I tucked it under my arm, holding it flat against my body, as if that might keep him from slipping away again.

Outside, the air felt different. Cooler. Quieter. The parking lot was nearly empty now, the day already beginning to close in on itself. I stood for a moment beside the car, keys in hand, and looked back at the building.

This place had once been the beginning. Nervous introductions. Hope dressed up as confidence. Two young people stepping into a life that still felt wide open.

And now it was the end.

I opened the car door and set his picture carefully on the seat beside me. When I pulled out of the lot, there was no rush, no urgency to get anywhere else. Just the steady movement forward, time continuing the way it always does.

The circle was complete.

Not neatly. Not gently. But fully.

And for the first time all day, I let myself sit with that truth and let the road carry me home.

Chapter 34

Room to Breathe

The house was still when I walked through the door.

Not empty. There were still flowers on every surface, still food covering the counters, but silent in a way it hadn't been in days.

There were no voices. No shuffling feet. No performative grief filling the air.

Just quiet.

I set my purse on the counter, then reached back into my bag and pulled out the framed photo from the funeral home. My father, smiling, from the first spring when he arrived at our house. I carried it into the formal room and placed it carefully on the coffee table, adjusting the angle until it faced the window.

I went back into the garage and lifted the clock urn from the passenger seat where I'd buckled it in, the seat belt crossed over it like a final act of care. It was heavier than it looked, dense in my hands, impossibly weighted for something that small. I carried it inside and set it beside the photograph.

I stood there for a moment, looking at the two of them together. Then I turned toward the kitchen.

I heard the ice maker clacking in the refrigerator, and somewhere in the house a clock ticked steadily, indifferent. I picked up a few glasses and mugs that had been abandoned that morning, still sitting on the kitchen table where guests had left them, and placed them in the sink. The ceramic clinked against the steel.

I opened the cabinet above the sink and pulled out a wine glass. Not the everyday kind. One of the good ones, thin-stemmed and delicate, reserved for celebrations or moments that mattered.

I reached for the Pinot Grigio in the fridge, the bottle perfectly chilled. The cork released with a delicate pop. I poured slowly, watching the pale gold liquid climb the glass, the light catching it just right.

I carried it to the formal room and sank into the chair I'd chosen years ago for exactly this reason. The way it cradled me. The way it faced the window so I could watch the world move without having to be part of it yet.

The first sip was cool and sharp, cutting through the heaviness in my chest. I closed my eyes and let it settle, feeling the tension in my shoulders begin to release, just slightly.

I lit a candle and glanced at his picture. The afternoon light was shifting, stretching long shadows across the yard. A neighbor walked past with a stroller. The maple tree swayed gently.

Everything was painfully ordinary.

Lilies still filled the air with their cloying sweetness. Food still crowded the counters. But the noise was gone.

And with the silence, I felt it again.

Relief.

Real and uncomplicated. Deep in my chest. I didn't think it would ever belong to me, and here it was. Just like the night he died.

And just like that night, there was no guilt, no accompanying shame. Just the pure, simple release that comes when you finally set down a weight you've been carrying so long you forgot what it felt like to walk without it.

Alzheimer's turns every caregiver into a sentinel. You don't rest. You patrol.

But sitting there in my chair, wine glass in hand, I realized with sudden, overwhelming clarity: there was nothing left to monitor.

It was over.

I could finally sleep.

The grief had already happened. It had been happening for years, stretched across every doctor's appointment and midnight wandering episode. I'd been mourning him long before he died. Mourning the man he used to be, the conversations we'd never have again, the memories that slipped away before I could catch them.

I sat there as the afternoon light shifted through the windows, turning from gold to gray, and let that truth settle.

And then, quietly, something else arrived alongside the relief.

Sadness.

Not for him. He was free now. Free from the confusion. Free from the fear. No more being trapped inside a mind that betrayed him.

The sadness was for me.

For the version of myself that disappeared while I stood guard. For the narrowing of my world. For the years spent surviving instead of living.

I let myself feel both.

The relief and the sadness, side by side, neither one canceling out the other. Both true. Both earned.

And then, in the space between them, something else arrived.

Possibility.

Not a promise. Not a plan. Just space.

Space to imagine mornings that didn't start with pill crushers and camera checks. Space to wonder what I might do with a day that belonged entirely to me.

I didn't have answers yet. I didn't need them.

I finally had room to ask the questions.

What did I want my life to look like now?

Who was I without the constant pull of caregiving?

What would I build in all this quiet?

I didn't know. But sitting there, with the light outside turning from gold to dusk, and the house finally still, I realized something important:

I had time to figure it out.

The paperwork would come. Mountains of it. Benefit claims to file. Accounts to close. His name removed from documents that had held it for decades. Calls that would drag me back into administrative hell, navigating systems designed to exhaust me, once again, into submission.

That was all ahead of me.

But in that moment, sitting in my quiet house with lilies I didn't ask for, and casseroles I wouldn't eat, all I knew was this:

My shift had ended.

For the first time in four years, I could close my eyes without fear.

I stood slowly, every muscle in my body protesting.

He wasn't suffering anymore.

And neither was I.

I climbed the stairs to my room, pulled off my uncomfortable clothes, and slid into bed. No cameras to check. No alarms to set. No listening for sounds that shouldn't be there.

Just sleep.

And tomorrow, when I woke up, I'd begin again.

Not as a caregiver.

As myself.

I didn't know who that was yet. Caregiving had blurred everything.

The lines between his life and mine.

Between devotion and depletion.

Between who I was and who I'd become.

But for the first time in years, I had permission to bring myself back into focus.

Afterword

To the Women Who Carry Everything

I started this book in a room designed for calm, facing everything inside of me that wasn't.

Clean lines surrounded me. A glass of wine sat beside the soft chair that held me. I stared into a mirror reflecting someone I barely recognized, and I listened.

I listened to the whisper of my father's voice that I didn't ask for and couldn't ignore.

Write it down.

So, I did.

I wrote it down. All of it. The chaos and the beauty sitting side by side. The sleepless nights. The quiet wishes I was afraid to say out loud. The locked doors and the escape routes. The strength that made me invisible. The love that nearly destroyed me.

If you've read this far, you know.

You know what it means to carry everything while disappearing inside the weight of it.

So, this is for you.

For the women who carry everything.

For the ones who stay when everyone else finds reasons to leave. Who hold the line when no one else even knows there's a line to hold. Who figure it out, again and again, without a manual, without training, without anyone telling them they're doing it right.

For the ones who fold the laundry between medication schedules. Who crush pills into applesauce. Who keep the appointments, track the insurance claims, fight with customer service reps who don't understand urgency, and still somehow remember to call their friends back even when they have nothing left to give.

For the ones who become the nurse, the therapist, the scheduler, the cook, the translator, the advocate, the emotional anchor, and still show up to work, raise children, lead meetings, build businesses, or try desperately to hold together a relationship with someone who never really sees how much weight they're carrying.

For the ones who ask for help and get silence in return.

For the ones who never ask because they've learned that asking only leads to disappointment.

For the ones who break down, but only when no one's watching. Only in the shower. Only in the car. Only in those stolen moments when they finally let themselves feel the full weight of what they've been holding.

You are not too much.

You are not weak.

You are not failing.

And you are not alone.

You are the threshold between chaos and order. The storm shelter when everything else falls apart. The quiet strength that holds generations together, even when no one notices the work it takes.

Here is what I have learned, what caregiving has burned into my bones as truth:

- You can love someone fiercely and still wish for their suffering to end.
- You can carry guilt and grace in the same breath without one erasing the other.
- Relief and grief are not opposites; they are companions.
- You do not need permission to rest.
- You do not need to earn ease.
- Wanting your life back does not make you selfish.
- Endurance looks different when you're the only one standing.

I didn't write this book to give you a checklist, a road map, or five easy steps to make everything better.

I wrote it to offer you a mirror.

Because somewhere out there is a woman sitting alone right now, convinced she's supposed to handle all of this without breaking. Convinced that asking for help means admitting failure. Convinced that if she just tries harder, pushes longer, sacrifices more, everything will somehow be okay.

Maybe that woman is you.

And maybe, just maybe, this is the moment you stop measuring your worth by how much you can endure.

You are strong. You were always strong.

But strength was never supposed to mean suffering alone.

It was never supposed to mean disappearing inside your own life.

It was never supposed to mean loving everyone else more than you love yourself.

So, here is your permission:

Permission to rest without guilt.

Permission to grieve what you've lost, including the parts of yourself you had to set down to pick up everyone else.

Permission to be angry at a system that asks everything of you and offers nothing in return.

Permission to want more than just survival.

Permission to imagine a life on the other side of this that includes joy, not just relief.

Permission to put yourself back on the list.

Not at the bottom.

At the top.

You have carried enough.

You have done enough.

You have been enough.

Now breathe. It is your birthright.

The woman in the mirror is still waiting.

She's been waiting for you to recognize her again.

To remember who you were before caregiving rewrote your entire story.

To reclaim the life that's still yours to build.

She's ready when you are.